THE AMERICANS WITH DISABILITIES ACT (ADA): OVERVIEW, REGULATIONS AND INTERPRETATIONS

THE AMERICANS WITH DISABILITIES ACT (ADA): OVERVIEW, REGULATIONS AND INTERPRETATIONS

NANCY LEE JONES

Novinka Books

New York

Senior Editors: Susan Boriotti and Donna Dennis
Coordinating Editor: Tatiana Shohov
Office Manager: Annette Hellinger
Graphics: Wanda Serrano and Matt Dallow
Editorial Production: Maya Columbus, Vladimir Klestov,
Matthew Kozlowski and Tom Moceri,
An and
Circulation: Ave Maria Gonzalez, Vera Popovic, Raymond Davis, Melissa Diaz
Magdalena Nuñez, Marlene Nuñez and Jeannie Pappas
Marketing: Cathy DeGregory
Communications and Acquisitions: Serge P. Shohov

Library of Congress Cataloging-in-Publication Data

Jones, Nancy Lee
The Americans with Disabilities Act (ADA): overview, regulations and interpretations /
Nancy Lee Jones.
p. cm.
Includes index.
ISBN: 1-59033-663-1 (softcover)
1. People with disabilities—Legal status, laws, etc.—United States. [DNLM 1. United
States. Americans with Disabilities Act of 1990. 2. Disabled Persons—legislation &
jurisprudence—United States. 3. Employment—legislation & jurisprudence—United States.
4. Health Services Accessibility—legislation & jurisprudence—United States. 5. Public
Policy—United States. HV 1553 J78a 2003] I. Title.

KF3738.J66 2003
342.73'087—dc21   2003005265

Copyright © 2003 by Novinka Books, An Imprint of
Nova Science Publishers, Inc.
400 Oser Ave, Suite 1600
Hauppauge, New York 11788-3619
Tele. 631-231-7269   Fax 631-231-8175
e-mail: Novascience@earthlink.net
Web Site: http://www.novapublishers.com

Printed in the United States of America

CONTENTS

PREFACE

The Americans with Disabilities Act (ADA) enacted on July 16, 1990, provides broad non-discrimination protection for individuals with disabilities in employment, public accommodations and services operated by public entities, transportation, and telecommunications. This book summarises the major provisions of the act as amended and discusses recent issues including rules, Supreme Court decisions, regulations and information sources.

Chapter 1

AMERICANS WITH DISABILITIES ACT (ADA) REQUIREMENTS CONCERNING THE PROVISION OF INTERPRETERS BY DOCTORS

Nancy Lee Jones

INTRODUCTION

The Americans with Disabilities Act (ADA), 42 U.S.C. §§ 12101 *et seq.,* prohibits discrimination against individuals with disabilities by places of public accommodations. A common question concerning the ADA is whether this prohibition requires medical doctors to provide an interpreter when they see a patient with a hearing disability. This requirement varies depending upon the situation presented but situations may arise where a doctor is obligated to provide an interpreter.

STATUTORY LANGUAGE

Title III of the ADA, section 302, 42 U.S.C. § 12182, provides generally that "[n]o individual shall be discriminated against on the basis of disability in the full and equal enjoyment of the goods, services, facilities, privileges, advantages, or accommodations of any place of public accommodation by any person who owns, leases (or leases to), or operates a place of public accommodation." In addition, this section provides that discrimination includes "a failure to make reasonable modifications in policies, practices, or procedures when such modifications are necessary to afford such goods, services, facilities, privileges, advantages, or accommodations to individuals with disabilities, unless the entity can demonstrate that making such modification would fundamentally alter the nature of such goods, services, facilities, privileges, advantages, or accommodations." The definition of public accommodation specifically includes the "professional office of a health care professional." 42 U.S.C. §12181(7)(F).

REGULATORY INTERPRETATION

The Department of Justice promulgated regulations to implement title III of the ADA on July 26, 1991. These regulations contain a provision on auxiliary aids and services. "A public accommodation shall take those steps that may be necessary to ensure that no individual with a disability is excluded, denied services, segregated or otherwise treated differently than other individuals because of the absence of auxiliary aids and services, unless the public accommodation can demonstrate that taking those steps would fundamentally alter the nature of the goods, services, facilities, privileges, advantages, or accommodations being offered or would result in an undue burden, *i.e.* significant difficulty or expense." 28 C.F.R. §36.303. The term auxiliary aids is further defined to include "qualified interpreters, notetakers, computer-aided transcription services, written materials..." *Id.*

The Department of Justice regulations stated that in determining whether an action is an undue burden various factors should be considered. These include: the nature and cost of the action, the overall financial resources of the site, the geographic separateness and the administrative or fiscal relationship of the sites in question to a parent corporation, the overall financial resources of the parent corporation, and the type of operation or operations of any parent corporation or entity. 28 C.F.R. §36.104.

The Department of Justice's analysis of its regulatory provisions when the regulations were proposed included as an example the situation where a note pad and written materials were insufficient to permit effective communication in a doctor's office when the matter to be discussed was major surgery. Commentators objected to this statement as conveying the impression that note pads were sufficient except in the most extreme circumstances. In its discussion of the final regulations, the Department of Justice observed that such a limitation was not intended. "Other situations may also require the use of interpreters to ensure effective communication depending on the facts of the particular case. It is not difficult to imagine a wide range of communications involving airs such as health, legal maters, and finances that would be sufficient lengthy or complex to require an interpreter for effective communication." 56 Fed. Reg. 35567 (July 26, 1991). In addition, the Department noticed that the use of a computer may be an intermediate step between an interpreter and a notepad. *Id.*

ANALYSIS

The ADA purposely adopted a flexible standard regarding nondiscrimination requirements. This flexibility was seen as allowing the nondiscrimination requirements to apply in the fairest manner to the myriad of circumstances presented by employers, public accommodations, and individuals with disabilities. However, this very flexibility means that precise requirements are not always readily enunciated. The answer then, to the question of whether a doctor must provide for a hearing impaired patient is dependent upon the particular circumstances.

There is some difficulty in narrowing the scope of such circumstance due to the paucity of judicial interpretations. The majority of the claims regarding the failure of a doctor to provide a hearing impaired patient with an interpreter have been resolved through either an informal or formal settlement process.[1] Generally, as mutual agreements between parties are not a matter of public record, the question of what particular circumstances warrant which auxiliary aids remain vague. However, there are some judicial decisions which provide guidance.

Effective Communication

As the regulations indicate, there is no absolute requirement that an interpreter be provided in a particular situation. One Key factual issue determining when there is such a requirement is whether other means may provide effective communication. In *Mayberry v. Van Valtier,* 843 F. Supp.

---

[1] The Department of Justice primarily tracks ADA claims to which they are a party. For information on settlement agreements on the ADA which have been negotiated by the Department of Justice see http://www.usdoj.gov/crt/ada/adahom1.htm.

1160 (E.D. Mich. 1994), the court found that a deaf Medicare patient was entitled to a trial on her claim that her doctor violated the ADA. The doctor had communicated with the patient for a number of years by passing notes or using one of the patient's children as an interpreter and on one occasion had noted in patient's file that her back pain was higher than she had originally thought and that this misunderstanding was "probably due to poor communications". The patient, Mrs. Mayberry, requested that the doctor provide an interpreter for a physical examination. The doctor complied but following the examination wrote a letter to the interpreter, with a copy to the patient stating that she would not be able to use the interpreter's services again and that "I really can't afford to take care of Mrs. Mayberry at all." The doctor characterized the letter as a protest against what was perceived as an unfair law. The court found that the allegations made were sufficient to reject a motion for summary judgment and ordered the case to proceed to trial. Subsequently, a judgment was rendered in favor of the doctor (Docket # 114 – May 22, 1995) but there is no record of a written opinion.

Physicians should also recognize that even if a deaf patient receives effective medical treatment, the doctor may still violate the ADA if the doctor did not "effectively communicate" with that patient. In *Aikins v. St. Helena Hospital,* 843 F. Supp. 1329 (N.D. Cal. 1994), the court found that adequate medical treatment does not defeat claims of failure to provide effective communication under the ADA and Rehabilitation Act of 1973.[2] Elaine Aikins, a hearing impaired individual and the California Association of the Deaf (CAD) alleged that St. Helena Hospital and Dr. James Lies failed to communicate effectively with Mrs. Aikins during her now deceased husband's medical treatment. The late Mr. Aikins was transported to St. Helena Hospital where Dr. Lies was responsible for his medical care. Mrs. Aikins requested an interpreter to facilitate communication with Dr. Lies. Instead of an interpreter the hospital provided Mrs. Aikins with an ineffective finger speller. Allegedly Mrs. Aikins was unable to effectively communicate with Dr. Lies or other hospital staff until her daughter became available to interpret. Mrs. Aikins and the CAD alleged that Dr. Lies and St. Helena Hospital violated both the ADA and the Rehabilitation Act. Dr. Lies maintained that Rehabilitation Act was inapplicable and St. Helena asserted that it complied with both the ADA and Rehabilitation Act. Although the case was later settled, the court noted that adequate medical treatment is not

---

[2] The Rehabilitation Act of 1973 prohibits entities receiving federal funds from discriminating against individuals on the basis of a disability. 29 U.S.C. § 794(a).

a defense to a claim that a defendant failed to provide effective communication under the Rehabilitation Act of 1973.

Citing *Aikins v. St. Helena Hospital, the court in Naiman v. New York University,* 1997 WL 249970 (S.D.N.Y.), 6 A.D. Cases 1345 (10 NDLR 39), found that a physician's effectiveness in providing medical treatment to a hearing impaired patient does not negate an ineffective communication claim under the ADA. Mr. Alec Naiman, who is hearing impaired, was admitted on several occasion to New York University Medical Center, operated by New York University. On each occasion Mr. Naiman requested interpreter. On one occasion the Center provided Mr. Naiman with a person minimally capable of communicating sign language. While on other visits Mr. Naiman alleged that the Center did not either provide an interpreter in a timely manner or did not provide an interpreter at all. Mr. Naiman contented that he needs an interpreter to participate in his medical care and is uncertain on his visits to the Center whether he will be able to effectively communicate with doctors and staff. New York University argued that Mr. Naiman failed to state a claim under the ADA because he received adequate medical care from the Medical Center. The court ruled in favor of the plaintiff, holding that a claim under ADA alleging ineffective communication relates to the patients exclusion from participation in their treatment and the treatment itself.

Undue Burden

The regulations also provide that an interpreter is not required if the doctor can demonstrate that doing so would fundamentally alter the nature of the goods, services, facilities, privileges, advantages, or accommodations being offered or would result in an undue burden. This issue was discussed in the recent case of *Bravin v. Mount Sinai Medical Center,* 1999 U.S. Dist. LEXIS 4915 (S.D.N.Y. 1999). The court there found that the hospital had alluded to an undue hardship but did not address the issue explicitly and therefore awarded summary judgment to the plaintiff.

Chapter 2

THE AMERICANS WITH DISABILITIES ACT: HIV INFECTION IS COVERED UNDER THE ACT

Nancy Lee Jones

INTRODUCTION

In *Bragdon v. Abbott,* No. 97-156 (June 25, 1998), the Supreme Court held that the respondent's asymptomatic HIV infection was a physical impairment impacting on the major life activity of reproduction thus rendering the HIV infection a disability under the Americans with Disabilities Act (ADA), 42 U.S.C. §§ 12101 *et seq.* The Court also examined the ADA's exception regarding a direct threat to the health or safety of others and found that courts should assess the objective reasonableness of the views of health care professionals by looking to the views of public health authorities but that these views could be rebutted by citing a credible scientific bases for deviating from the accepted norm. *Bragdon* was remanded for further proceedings regarding the question or risk.

Bragdon v. Abbott has been heralded as a significant decision advancing the rights of individuals who have asymptomatic HIV infection. It also has broader implications on the ADA coverage of reproductive disabilities.

BACKGROUND

In 1994 Dr. Bragdon performed a dental examination on Ms. Abbott and discovered a cavity. Ms. Abott had indicated on her registration form that she was HIV positive. At that time, she was asymptomatic. Dr. Bragdon told her that he would not fill her cavity in his office but would treat her only in a hospital setting. This would have resulted in higher costs for Ms. Abbott since, although Dr. Bragdon would have charged his regular free, she would have had to have paid the hospital costs. Ms. Abbott did not find this acceptable and filed a complaint under the ADA, a broad civil rights statute that prohibits discrimination against individuals with disabilities. She prevailed at the district court and court of appeals levels and at the Supreme Court on the issue of whether she was an individual with a disability but the case was remanded for further consideration regarding the issue of direct threat.

THE AMERICAN WITH DISABILITIES ACT

The Americans with Disabilities Act provides broad nondiscrimination protection for individuals with disabilities in employment, public services, public accommodation and services operated by private entities, transpiration and telecommunication.[1] The ADA states that "the term 'disability' means, with respect to an individual – (A) a physical or mental impairment that substantially limits one or more of the major life activities of such individuals; (B) a record of such an impairment; or (C) being regarded as having such an impairment."[2] Although discrimination against such individuals is prohibited in places of public accommodations such as doctor's offices,[3] there are some limitations on the reach of this nondiscrimination requirement. The most significant of these limitations with regard to the issues presented by *Bragdon* is the exception for situations that pose a direct threat to the health or safety of others. The term "direct threat" is defined in the statute as "a significant risk to the health or safety of others that cannot be eliminated by a modification of policies, practices, or

---

[1] For a more detailed discussion of the ADA see Jones, "The Americans with Disabilities Act (ADA): An Overview of Major Provisions and Issues," CRS Rep. No. 97-242A (Feb. 12, 1997).

[2] 42 U.S.C. §12102(2).

[3] 42 U.S.C. §12181.

procedures or by the provision of auxiliary aids or services."[4] It was created in an attempt to differentiate legitimate public health concerns from prejudicial stereotypes.

SUPREME COURT'S DECISION

The Supreme Court held that Ms. Abbott's asymptomatic HIV infection was a physical impairment impacting on the major life activity of reproduction thus rendering the HIV infection a disability under the ADA. In addition, the Court held that when interpreting the ADA, courts should assess the objective reasonableness of the views of health care professionals by looking to the views of public health authorities but that these views could be rebutted by citing a credible scientific bases for deviating from the accepted norm and remanded *Bragdon* for further consideration on this issues. These holdings were reached in a 5 to 4 decision, with Justice Kennedy writing for the majority. Justices Stevens and Breyer joined in a concurring opinion and Justice Ginsburg filed a separate concurring opinion. Chief Justice Rehnquist, joined by Justices Scalia and Thomas, filed an opinion concurring in part and dissenting in part. Justice O'Connor filed a separate opinion concurring in part and dissenting in part.

Definition of Individual with a Disability

Writing for the majority, Justice Kennedy began by examining the issue of whether asymptomatic HIV infection constitutes a disability under the ADA, parsing the statutory language and finding that Ms. Abbott was covered under subsection (A) – having a physical or mental impairment that substantially limits one or more major life activities. In reaching this holding, Justice Kennedy used the following analytic framework: first, determining whether Ms. Abbott's HIV infection was a physical impairment; second, determining the life activity affected and whether it constituted a major life activity; and, third, determining whether the impairment substantially limited the major life activity. He then noted that the ADA's definition was "drawn almost verbatim from the definition of 'handicapped individual' included in the Rehabilitation Act" and that the ADA specifically

---

[4] *Id.*

states that the ADA shall not be construed to apply a lesser standard than the standards applied under title V of the Rehabilitation Act and its regulations.[5]

The first question Justice Kennedy examined was whether Ms. Abbott's asymptomatic HIV infection constituted a physical impairment. After a detailed clinical discussion of HIV infection, Justice Kennedy concluded that "in light of the immediacy with which the virus begins to damage the infected person's white blood cells and the severity of the disease, we hold it is an impairment from the moment of infection." Next, Justice Kennedy turned to the issue of whether the physical impairment affected a major life activity. Ms. Abbott had argued that her HIV infection placed a substantial limitation on her ability to reproduce and to bear children and Justice Kennedy had "little difficulty" concluding that reproduction was a major life activity since "reproduction and the sexual dynamics surrounding it are central to the life process itself." The ADA was found not to be limited to the aspects of a person's life which have a public, economic or daily character. The breadth of the term "major" "confounds the attempt to limit its construction in this manner."

The final issue regarding the definition of individual with a disability was whether Ms. Abbott's physical impairment was a substantial limitation on the major life activity of reproduction. After an evaluation of the medial evidence, Justice Kennedy concluded that Ms. Abbott's ability to reproduce was substantially limited in two ways: (1) an attempt to conceive would impose a significant risk on Ms. Abbott's partner, and (2) an HIV infected woman risks infecting her child during gestation and childbirth.

Justice Kennedy found that the reasoning used above to find that asymptomatic HIV infection was a physical impairment that placed a substantial limitation on a major life activity was confirmed by consistent agency and judicial interpretation. He noted that "every agency to consider the issue under the Rehabilitation Act found statutory coverage for persons with asymptomatic HIV." The legislative history of he ADA, which cited the section 504 interpretations, was also seen as buttressing the Court's conclusion. In addition, the administrative guidance issued for the ADA was found to indicate that asymptomatic HIV infection should be covered.

---

[5] Section 504 of the Rehabilitation, 29 U.S.C. §794, prohibits discrimination against otherwise qualified individuals with disabilities in any program or activity receiving federal financial assistance, the executive agencies or the U.S. Postal Service. Section 504 and its regulations served as a model for the ADA which expanded these protections to entities that did not receive federal funds.

Direct Threat Exception

The other major issue addressed by the Court in *Bragdon* involved the interpretation of the ADA's direct thereat exception. Even with the finding that Ms. Abbott was an individual with a disability, Dr. Bragdon could have refused to treat her or insisted on treating her in a different setting if her condition "pose[d] a direct threat to the health or safety of others."[6] Direct threat is defined in the ADA as "a significant risk to the health or safety of others that cannot be eliminated by a modification of policies, practices, or procedures or by the provision of auxiliary aids or services."[7] After examining the Court's decision in *School Board of Nassau County v. Arline*, 480 U.S. 273 (1987), Justice Kennedy determined that "the existence, or nonexistence, of a significant risk must be determined from the standpoint of the person who refuses the treatment or accommodation, and the risk assessment must be based on medical or other objective evidence." Dr. Bragdon had the duty to assess the risk of infection "based on the objective, scientific information available to him and others in his profession. His belief that a significant risk existed, even if maintained in good faith, would not relieve him from liability." Thus, there was no special deference accorded to Dr. Bragdon because of his professional status.

The question remained as to how to determine if Dr. Bragdon's actions were reasonable. Justice Kennedy observed that "in assessing the reasonableness of petitioner's actions, the views of public health authorities, such as the U.S. Public Health Service, CDC, and the National Institutes of Health, are of special weight and authority." However, Justice Kennedy found that the views of these entities were not necessarily determinative and could be refuted by citing a credible scientific basis for differing from the accepted norm. The Court of Appeals determination of this issue was examined and found to have placed mistaken reliance in the CDC Dentistry Guidelines and the 1991 American Dental Association Policy on HIV.[8] The Supreme Court remanded the case for further consideration on this issue. "We conclude that the proper course is to give the Court of Appeals the opportunity to determine whether our analysis of some of the studies cited by

---

[6] 42 U.S.C. §1212(b)(3).

[7] *Id.*

[8] The CDC Guidelines recommend certain universal precautions but do not assess the level of risk. The American Dental Association Policy on HIV is not that of a public health authority and Justice Kennedy observed that it was not clear the extent to which the policy was based on an assessment of ethical and professional duties and the extent to which the policy was based on a scientific assessment of the risk.

the parties would change its conclusion that petitioner presented neither objective evidence nor a triable issue of fact on the question of risk."

Concurring Opinions

Two concurring opinions were filed: one by Justice Stevens who was joined by Justice Breyer and one by Justice Ginsburg. Justice Stevens wrote that he would have preferred an outright affirmance of the Court of Appeals decision but joined with Justice Kennedy to provide a majority opinion. Justice Ginsburg agreed with the majority and stated that "No rational legislator, it seems to me apparent, would require nondiscrimination once symptoms become visible but permit discrimination when the disease, though present is not yet visible."

Dissenting Opinions

Chief Justice Rehnquist, joined by Justices Scalia and Thomas, dissented in part and concurred in part. He dissented from the majority, finding that Ms. Abbott had failed to demonstrate that any of her major life activities were substantially limited by her HIV infection. First, it was noted that the issue of whether reproduction is a major life activity should be answered with regard to the individual in question and he further observed that there was no evidence, that absent the HIV infection, Ms. Abbott would have had or considered having children. Second, the Chief Justice found that reproduction was not a major life activity since reproduction is not essential in the day-to-day existence of a normally functioning individual. And, even if reproduction was a major life activity, the dissent found that asymptomatic HIV infection does not substantially limit that activity. The Chief Justice concurred in the remand on the direct threat issue but disagreed with the majority with regard to its conclusion that the views of public health officials are entitled to special weight. He observed that "the credentials of the scientists employed by the public health authority, and the soundness of their studies, must stand on their own."

Justice O'Connor wrote a separate opinion, dissenting in part and concurring in part. She agreed with the dissenting opinion of the Chief Justice that Ms. Abbott's claim of disability should be evaluated on an individualized basis and that Ms. Abbott did not prove that her asymptomatic HIV infection substantially limited one or more of her major life activities.

Justice O'Connor also agreed with the decision to remand on the direct threat issue.

IMPLICATIONS

Bragdon has implications for other legal issues beyond its basic holding that Ms. Abbott's asymptomatic HIV infection is a disability under the ADA. Prior to the Court's decision, the courts of appeal had been split on the issue of whether reproduction is a major life activity.[9] In arriving at its holding, the Court specifically found that reproduction was a major life activity thus resolving this issue. In addition, the Court's holding that asymptomatic HIV infection is covered under the ADA, would appear to indicate that asymptomatic conditions may also be covered. For example, in *Ryan v. Grae & Rybicki P.C.,* 135 F.3d 867 (2d Cir. 1998), the second circuit held that a woman with ulcerative colitis was not an individual with a disability since she was asymptomatic most of the time. However, the majority's language regarding "the immediacy with which the virus begins to damage the infected person's white blood cells" may create a standard which might not be met by all asymptomatic conditions.

The Court also provided a framework for future analysis of issues involving the first prong of the definition of disability. First, a court is to determine whether a condition is a physical impairment; second, the life activity affected and whether this is a major life activity are to be determined and; third, a determination shall be made concerning whether the impairment substantially limits the major life activity.

The Supreme Court remanded the case to the first circuit for further consideration of the issue of what constitutes a direct threat under the ADA. Although the majority found that there was no special deference accorded to Dr. Bragdon because of his professional status, the question of how to determine if his actions were reasonable was less clear. The decision of the first circuit on remand, will be significant in determining this issue.

---

[9] See e.g., *Krauel v. Iowa Methodist Medical Center,* 95 F.3d 694 (8th Cir. 1996) (Finding that the ability to reproduce is not a major life activity).

Chapter 3

THE AMERICANS WITH DISABILITIES ACT AND RIGHTS TO COMMUNITY CARE: *OLMSTEAD V. L.C.*

Nancy Lee Jones

INTRODUCTION

The Supreme Court granted certiorari on December 14, 1998 in *Olmstead v. L.C.* to address the issue of whether the public services portion of the Americans with Disabilities Act (ADA) compels the state of Georgia to provide treatment for the plaintiff mentally disabled persons in community placement when such treatment could be provided in a state mental institution.

BACKGROUND

The Americans with Disabilities Act, 42 U.S.C. §§12101 *et seq.,* provides broad nondiscrimination protection for individuals with disabilities in employment, public services, public accommodations and services operated by public entities, transportation, and telecommunications. More specifically, at 42 U.S.C. §12132 the ADA prohibits discrimination against persons with disabilities in the provision of public services by state and local governments. The Department of Justice has promulgated regulations which state that a "public entity shall administer services, programs, and activities in the most integrated setting appropriate to the needs of qualified individuals with disabilities."[1] In April 1998 the court of appeals for the eleventh circuit held that the ADA and its regulations prohibited a state from confining disabled individuals in state run institutions when those individuals could be appropriately treated in a more integrated community setting.[2] The Supreme Court granted certiorari on December 14, 1998.

COURT OF APPEALS DECISION

L.C. by Zimring v. Olmstead, supra, was an action brought by two patients housed in a state psychiatric hospital challenging their continued confinement as a failure to provide care in the most integrated setting appropriate and thus violating the ADA. The plaintiffs prevailed on a summary judgment in the district court and the case was then appealed to the eleventh circuit which affirmed the district court's decision.

The State argued that the district court's application of the statutory and regulatory language was contrary to the requirement of the ADA that the discrimination against an individual with a disability be "by reason of such disability." The State contended that the plaintiffs did not show that they were denied community placements available to individuals without disabilities because of disability since such placements were not provided for individuals without disabilities. The court of appeals observed that, "reduced to its essence, the State's argument is that Title II of the ADA affords no protection to individuals with disabilities who receive public services designed only for individuals with disabilities." The court of appeals examined the statutory language and the regulations set forth above and found that "by definition, where, as here, the State confines an individual with a disability in an institutionalized setting when a community placement is appropriate, the State has violated the core principle underlying the ADA's integration mandate." At 897. In addition, the legislative history of the ADA and the history of section 504 of the Rehabilitation Act of 1973, 29 U.S.C. §794, were examined and found to support the holding of the district court.

---

[1] 28 C.F.R. §35. 130(d).

[2] *L.C. by Zimring v. Olmstead,* 138 F.3d 893 (11th Cir. 1998). A similar case in the third circuit reached the same conclusion. See *Helen L. v. DiDario,* 46 F.3d 325 (3d Cir. 1995), *cert. denied, sub nom. Pennsylvania Secretary of Public Welfare v. Idell,* 516 U.S. 813 (1995).

The court of appeals also rejected the State's claim that the denial of community placement was due to the State's lack of funds, not the plaintiff's disabilities. The court observed that the ADA does not require the State to provide services if these services would require a fundamental alteration in its programs. However, in the situation presented, the court found that there was not sufficient evidence to make a determination of whether the services sought would require a fundamental alteration and so remanded this issue to the district court for further proceedings.

The limited nature of its ruling was also emphasized by the court. *Olmstead* was not a class action suit and applied only to the two individuals who had shown that they were qualified for a community based program. In addition, the court of appeals specifically stated: "We emphasize that our holding does not mandate the deinstitutionalization of individuals with disabilities. Instead, we hold that where, as here, a disabled individual's treating professionals find that a community-based placement is appropriate for that individual, the ADA imposes a duty to provide treatment in a community setting – the most integrated setting appropriate to that patient's needs. Where there is no such finding, on the other hand, nothing in the ADA requires the deinstitutionalization of that patient." At 902.

IMPLICATIONS

Despite the court of appeal's limiting language, the decision of the eleventh circuit in *Omstead* has led to significant controversy. Twenty two states and the territory of Guam filed an amicus brief with the Supreme Court asking the Court to review the eleventh circuit's decision and stating that "the broad-ranging impact on the states of the Eleventh Circuit's holding cannot be underestimated ...."[3] This brief contended that the eleventh circuit's opinion had been "relied upon in several lawsuits designed to reshape the manner in which services (not provided to nondisabled persons) are provided by the states to individuals with disabilities."[4] In addition, the brief argued that the eleventh circuit's decision has a "profound" impact on

---

[3] The twenty two states are Florida, Alabama, California, Colorado, Delaware, Hawaii, Louisiana, Maryland, Michigan, Mississippi, Montana, Nebraska, Nevada, New Hampshire, Pennsylvania, South Carolina, South Dakota, Tennessee, Texas, Utah, West Virginia, and Wyoming.

[4] Amicus Curiae Brief of the States of Florida, et al., in support of petitioners, On Petition for a Writ of Certiorari, No 98-536, at 1 (Bold in original).

the provision of services in various contexts and would impose a significant cost burden.

Disability advocates have agreed that the decision by the Supreme Court could be significant but differ on the possible meaning of the decision. An attorney who was involved in a similar lawsuit in Pennsylvania[5] was quoted as stating: "This will be the defining moment for the ADA." He went on to state that "if the Supreme Court rules in favor of Georgia, the ADA will become a mere shell of what it is intended to be, stripping away its major civil rights provision – integration."[6]

The Supreme Court's decision will be only the fourth ADA case decided by the Court[7] although the Court currently has granted certiorari in four other ADA cases in addition to *Olmstead.*[8] The decision on *Olmstead* could be a

---

[5] *Helen L. v. DiDario,* 46 F.3d 325 (3d Cir. 1995), *cert. den. sub nom. Pennsylvania Secretary of Public Welfare v. Idell S.,* 516 U.S. 813 (1995).

[6] Michael Auberger, "Disability Rights Group Says Governors Declare War on Disabled People," *U.S. Newswire* (Dec. 18, 1998).

[7] In 1998, the Supreme Court decided three ADA cases: *Pennsylvania Department of Prisons v. Yeskey,* _U.S._, 118 S.Ct. 1952, 141 L.Ed.2d.215 (1998); *Bragdon v. Abbott,* _U.S._, 118 S.Ct.2196, 141 L.Ed.2d 40 (1998); *Wright v. Universal Maritime Service Corp.,* _U.S._ 119 S.Ct.391, 142 L.Ed.2d 361 (1998).

[8] *Cleveland v. Policy Mgmt. Systems,* _U.S._, 119 S.Ct. 39; 142 L.Ed. 30 (Oct. 5, 1998) (Whether application for or receipt of disability insurance benefits under the Social security Act creates a rebuttable presumption that the application or recipient is judicially estopped from asserting that she is a qualified individual with a disability); *Murphy v. United Parcel Service, Inc.,* _U.S._ (January 8, 1999)(Whether petitioner's hypertension should be evaluated in its unmedicated state); *Sutton v. United Air Lines, Inc.,* _U.S._ (January 8, 1999) (When airline pilot's uncorrected vision is so poor that it constitutes physical impairment under the ADA, is the pilot nevertheless excluded from protection

major ADA decision if the Supreme Court decides the case on the issues relating to the requirement of integration. Although the Court could emphasize the limited nature of the eleventh circuit's decision, it is probably unlikely that it will avoid the issues in this manner. It is somewhat unusual for the Supreme Court to grant certiorari in a case like *Omstead* where there is no conflict between various judicial circuits and when this occurs, the Supreme Court often reverses the lower court's decision. Whether this will be the situation in *Olmstead* remains to be seen.

---

under the act if her vision can be corrected); *Albertson Inc. v. Kirkingburg,* _U.S._ (January 8, 1999)(Whether an individual with monocular vision is an individual with a disability under the ADA).

Chapter 4

THE AMERICANS WITH DISABILITIES ACT (ADA) IN THE SUPREME COURT: DECIDED AND PENDING CASES

Nancy Lee Jones

INTRODUCTION

Although the Americans with Disabilities Act (ADA) was enacted in 1990, cases involving the Act were decided by the Supreme Court for the first time in 1998. These cases were *Bragdon v. Abbott,* involving HIV infection, *Pennsylvania Department of Prisons v. Yeskey,* involving ADA coverage of state prisons, and *Wright v. Universal Maritime Service Corp.,* involving arbitration clauses and the ADA. Since the rulings on the first three cases, the Supreme Court has granted certiorari in five other cases involving the ADA, one of which was decided in May 24, 1999. The Supreme Court's decisions in these cases could have a major impact on the interpretation of the law, especially concerning issues involving the definition of disability and the requirement for integrated settings.

BACKGROUND

The Americans with Disabilities Act, 42 U.S.C. §§12101 *et seq.,* provides broad nondiscrimination protection for individuals with disabilities in employment, public services, public accommodations and services operated by public entities, transportation, and telecommunications. Enacted in 1990, the ADA is a civil rights statute that has as its purpose "to provide a clear and comprehensive national mandate for the elimination of discrimination against individuals with disabilities."[1] It has been the subject of numerous lower court decisions which are just beginning to be considered by the Supreme Court. Since 1998, the Supreme Court has decided four cases involving the ADA and will consider four more cases before the end of the term.

DECIDED CASES

The most significant of the ADA cases decided by the Supreme Court to date is *Bragdon v. Abbott* where the Supreme Court, in a case involving a dentist who refused to treat an HIV infected individual outside of a hospital, addressed the ADA definition of individual with a disability.[2] In *Bragdon,* the Court found that the plaintiff's asymptomatic HIV infection was a physical impairment impacting on the major life activity of reproduction thus rending HIV infection a disability under the ADA. The Court also dealt with the issue of the application of the ADA's direct threat provision. The ADA does not require that an entity permit an individual to participate in or benefit from the services of a public accommodation where such an individual poses a direct threat to the health or safety of others.[3] The Court determined that there is a duty to assess the risk of infection "based on the objective, scientific information available" and that a "belief that a significant risk existed, even if maintained in good faith, would not relieve him from liability." The Court remanded the case for consideration of the weight to be given to various pieces of evidence relating to the direct threat issue and on remand the court of appeals for the first circuit concluded that the defendant had produced no legitimate scientific evidence to show that providing

---

[1] 42 U.S.C. §12102(b)(1).

[2] 524 U.S. 624 (1998). For a more detailed discussion of this decision see Jones, "The Americans with Disabilities Act: HIV Infection is Covered Under the Act," CRS Report 98-599 (July 10, 1998).

[3] 42 U.S.C. §12182(b)(3).

routine dental care would subject him to a significant risk of contacting HIV.[4] The Supreme Court denied certiorari on May 24, 1999.[5]

In *Pennsylvania Department of Prisons v. Yeskey,*[6] the Court found that state prisons were covered under title II of the ADA. The state had argued that state prisoners were not covered since such coverage would "alter the usual constitutional balance between the States and Federal Government." The Supreme Court rejected this argument, observing that "the ADA plainly covers state institutions *without* any exception that could cast the coverage of prisons into doubt."

In *Wright v. Universal Maritime Service Corp.,*[7] a unanimous Court held that the general arbitration clause in a collective bargaining agreement does not require a plaintiff to use the arbitration procedure for an alleged violation of the ADA. The Court's decision was limited since it did not find it necessary to reach the issue of the validity of a union-negotiated waiver. In other words, the Court found that a general arbitration agreement is a collective bargaining agreement is not sufficient to waive rights under civil rights statutes. However, the Court did not reach situations where collective bargaining agreements are very specific in requiring arbitration for alleged violations of civil rights statutes.

The relationship between the receipt of SSDI benefits and the ability of an individual to pursue an ADA claim was the issue in *Cleveland v. Policy Management Systems Corp.*[8] The Supreme Court unanimously held that pursuit and receipt of SSDI benefits does not automatically estop a recipient from pursuing an ADA claim or even create a strong presumption against success under the ADA. Observing that the Social Security Act and the ADA both help individuals with disabilities but in different ways, the Court found that "despite the appearance of conflict that arises from the language of the two statutes, the two claims do not inherently conflict to the point where courts should apply a special negative presumption like the one applied by the Court of Appeals here." The fact that the ADA defines a qualified individuals as one who can perform the essential functions of the job with or without reasonable accommodation was seen as a key distinction between the ADA and the Social Security Act. In addition, the Court observed that SSDI benefits are sometimes granted to individuals who are working.

---

[4] *Abbott v. Bragdon,* 1998 U.S. App. LEXIS 32708(Dec. 29, 1998).
[5] 1999 U.S. LEXIS 3475 (May 24, 1999).
[6] 524 U.S. 206 (1998).
[7] _U.S., 119 S.Ct. 391, 142 L.Ed.2d 361 (1998).
[8] _U.S., 1999 U.S. LEXIS 3452 (May 24, 1999).

However, although these distinctions between the two statutes would rule out a special legal presumption, the Court did note that in some cases an earlier SSDI claim may genuinely conflict with an ADA claim. Therefore, if an individual has asserted that he or she is unable to work in an application for SSDI benefits, this may negate the ADA requirement that the individual with a disability be able to perform the essential functions of the job. For that reason the Court held that "an ADA plaintiff cannot simply ignore the apparent contradiction that arises out of the earlier SSDI total disability claim. Rather, she must proffer a sufficient explanation." Since the parties to the case in *Cleveland* did not have the opportunity to examine the plaintiffs contentions in court, the case was vacated and remanded for further proceedings.

PENDING CASES

As of May 25, 1999 the Supreme Court has four ADA cases pending. Three of the pending cases involve issues relating to the definition of disability. The other one involves issues relating to community placement.

The Court granted certiorari on December 14, 1998 in *Olmstead v. L.C.* to address the issue of whether the public services title of the ADA compels the state of Georgia to provide treatment for the plaintiff mentally disabled persons in community placement when such treatment could be provided in a state mental institution.[9] The eleventh circuit court of appeals held that the ADA and its regulations prohibited a state from confining the plaintiffs in state run institutions when those individuals could be appropriately treated in a more integrated community setting.[10] The court of appeals was careful to limit its holding, stating that it was not a class action suit and applied only to the two individuals who had shown that they were qualified for a community based program. The eleventh circuit also stated: "We emphasize that our holding does not mandate the deinstitutionalization of individuals with disabilities. Instead we hold that where, as here, a disabled individual's treating professionals find that a community-based placement is appropriate for that individual, the ADA imposes a duty to provide treatment in a community setting – the most integrated setting appropriate to that patient's needs. Where there is no such finding, on the other hand, nothing in the

---

[9] _U.S., 119 S.Ct. 617, 67 U.S.L.W. 3392, 3408 (1998). For a more detailed discussion of this case see Jones, "The Americans with Disabilities Act and Rights to Community Care: *Olmstead v. L.C.,*" CRS Report RS20029 (January 25, 1999).

[10] *L.C. by Zimring v. Olmstead,* 138 F.Sd 893 (11ᵗʰ Cir. 1998).

ADA requires the deinstitutionalization of that patient."[11] Despite this limiting language, the decision of the eleventh circuit has led to considerable controversy and twenty two states and the territory of Guam filed an amicus brief with the Supreme Court asking the Court to review the decision stating that "the broad-ranging impact on the states of the Eleventh Circuit's holding cannot be underestimated."[12]

The other three cases the Supreme Court is to decide all involve issues relating to the definition of disability. Two of these cases, *Murphy v. United Parcel Service, Inc.* and *Sutton v. Untied Air Lines, Inc.,* involve the issue of whether the effects of medication or assistive devices should be taken into consideration in determining whether or not an individual has a disability. The Equal Employment Opportunities Commission (EEOC) has taken the position that whether or not an individual has a disability should be determined by what their condition would be without medication or an assistive device. *Murphy* and *Sutton* have taken the opposite view. In *Sutton,* the tenth circuit held that United Airlines did not violate the ADA when it denied jobs to twins who had uncorrected vision of 20/200 and 20/400. Both of the twins were commercial airline pilots for regional commuter airlines and had 20/20 vision with corrective lenses. However, United rejected their applications based on its policy of requiring uncorrected vision of 20/100 or better for its pilots. The tenth circuit noted that the twin's vision was a physical impairment but found that because it was corrected, they were not substantially impaired in the major life activity of seeing. The Supreme Court granted certiorari on three issues: (1) when an airlines pilot's vision is so poor it constitutes a physical impairment under the ADA, is the pilot excluded from coverage if her vision is correctable, (2) should courts defer to the EEOC's guidance that disabilities should be analyzed in their uncorrected state, and (3) is a commercial pilot regarded as disabled by a major airline that refuses to employ her as a pilot due to poor vision?[13]

In *Murphy* the tenth circuit relied on its ruling is *Sutton* to find that a former truck mechanic with high blood pressure was not an individual with a disability since he experiences no substantial limitations in major life activities while he takes his medication. The Supreme Court granted certiorari on two questions: (1) does the ADA require that the plaintiff's hypertension be evaluated in its unmedicated state and (2) was there no

---

[11] *Id.* At 902.
[12] Amicus Curiae Brief of the States of Florida et al., in support of petitioners for a Writ of Certiorari, No. 98-536, at 1.
[13] 525 U.S. _, 142 L.Ed.2d 653, 67 U.S.L.W. 3433 (January 8, 1999).

genuine dispute about whether the defendant regarded the plaintiff as disabled and fired him due to his hypertension?[14]

The third ADA case involving the definition of a disability, *Albertsons Inc. v. Kirkingburg, Hallie,* concerns a truck driver with monocular vision. The ninth circuit court of appeals held that the plaintiff was an individual with a disability under the ADA.[15] The plaintiff's vision is 20/200 in one eye and uncorrectable; his other eye is correctable to 20/40. He obtained a waiver of the Department of Transportation (DOT) vision standards but the defendant refused to accept the waiver. The ninth circuit found that the defendant could not selectively adopt or reject the Department of Transportation's safety standards. The Supreme Court granted certiorari on three questions: (1) is an individual with monocular vision disabled under the ADA, (2) is a commercial vehicle driver with monocular vision who failed to meet the minimum DOT vision requirements a qualified individual under the ADA, and (3) must an employer adopt an experimental vision waiver program as a means of reasonable accommodation?[16]

---

[14] 525 U.S. _, 142 L.Ed.2d 653, 67 U.S.L.W. 3433 (January 8, 1999).
[15] 14 F.3d 1228 (9th Cir. 1998).
[16] 525 U.S. _, 142 L.Ed.2d 654, 67 U.S.L.W. 3433 (January 8, 1999).

Chapter 5

The Americans with Disabilities Act: Equal Employment Opportunity Commission Regulations for Individuals with Disabilities

Nancy Lee Jones

Introduction

The Equal Employment Opportunities Commission (EEOC) has recently promulgated final regulations under title I of the Americans with Disabilities Act, which prohibits discrimination against individuals with disabilities. With regard to employment, the ADA essentially provides that no covered entity shall discriminate against a qualified individual with a disability because of the disability in regard to job application procedures, the hiring, advancement, or discharge of employees, employee compensation, job training and other terms, conditions and privileges of employment. Title I of the ADA and the EEOC regulations will go into effect for employers who employ more than 25 employees on July 26, 1992. For employers who employ 15 or more employees, the effective date will be July 26, 1994.

The EEOC's ADA regulations closely parallel the statutory language of the ADA, its legislative history, and regulatory and judicial interpretation of section 504 of the Rehabilitation Act of 1973. The regulations do provide more detailed guidance in certain areas, for example with the definition of "essential functions," the definition of individual with disabilities, and the definition of direct threat. However, the regulations have been criticized as failing to provide sufficient specific guidance in other areas. This issue has been raised generally concerning the case-by-case approach delineated in the regulations and more specifically regarding issues raised by collective bargaining agreements, insurance, and worker's compensation. EEOC has noted that it will issue a compliance manual if February 1992 which may address some of these issues.

BACKGROUND

The Americans with Disabilities Act (ADA) is a major civil rights statute covering individuals with disabilities. Final regulations have recently been promulgated concerning employment issues by the Equal Employment Opportunities Commission (EEOC) for title I of the ADA. Title I of the ADA, and these regulations, will go into effect for employers who employ more than 25 employees on July 26, 1992. For employers who employ 15 or more employees, the effective date will be July 26, 1994. The EEOC regulations provide significant guidance for compliance but have been criticized for aspects of their interpretation of the statute and for failure to provide sufficient guidance in certain areas.

The ADA, P.L 101-336, 42 U.S.C. §§ 12101 et seq., has often been described as the most sweeping nondiscrimination legislation since the Civil Rights Act of 1964. Enacted on July 26, 1990, it provides broad based nondiscrimination protection for individuals with disabilities in employment, public services, public accommodations and services operated by private entities, transportation, and telecommunications. The act specifically provides for the issuance of regulations by various entities and five major sets of regulations have been promulgated: accessibility guidelines by the Architectural and Transportation Barriers Compliance Board[1], regulations for nondiscrimination on the basis of disability by public accommodations

---

[1] 56 Fed. Reg. 35408 (July 26, 1991). Copies of these regulations may be obtained from the Architectural and Transportation Barriers Compliance Board, 111 18th St. N.W. Suite 501, Washington, D.C. 20036; 202-653-7834 – Voice/TDD.

by the Department of Justice[2], regulations for nondiscrimination on the basis of disability in state or local government services by the Department of Justice[3], regulations concerning equal employment opportunity for individuals with disabilities by the EEOC,[4] and regulations concerning transportation. [5]

STATUTORY REQUIREMENTS OF THE ADA REGARDING EMPLOYMENT

Section 106 of the ADA, 42 U.S.C. § 12116, requires the EEOC to issue regulations implementing title I of the Act within one year of the act's passage. Proposed regulations were issued on February 28, 1991 and final regulations were promulgated on July 26, 1991.

The ADA is a detailed statute which is described by the EEOC as "unusual... in that it contains a level of detail more commonly found in regulations, leaving very little room for regulatory discretion... The regulation merely explains and provides guidance on the statutory requirements by relying primarily on existing case law, which is another limitation on Commission discretion in constructing the regulation."[6] Prior to a discussion of the regulations, therefore, it is helpful to examine briefly the ADA's statutory language and legislative history regarding title I.

The Americans with Disabilities Act was based on the regulations and Judicial interpretation of section 504 of the Rehabilitation Act of 1973, 29 U.S.C. sec. 794.[7] The definition of the term "disability" is the same as that applicable to section 504: the term disability is defined as meaning with respect to an individual "(A) a physical or mental impairment that substantially limits one or more of the major life activities of such

---

[2] 56 Fed. Reg. 35544 (July 26, 1991). Copies of these regulations may be obtained from the Department of Justice, P.O. Box 66118, Washington, D.C. 20530-6118; 202-514-0301 (Voice); 202-514-0381 (TDD).

[3] 56 Fed. Reg. 35694 (July 26, 1991). Copies of these regulations may be obtained from the Department of Justice, P.O. Box 66118, Washington, D.C. 20530-6118; 202-514-0301 (Voice); 202 –514-0381 (TDD).

[4] 56 Fed. Reg. 35726 (July 26, 1991). Copies of these regulations can be obtained from the Equal Employment Opportunity Commission, 1801 L St. N.W. Room 9024, Washington, D.C. 20507; 202-663-4900 (Voice); 202-663-4399 (TDD).

[5] 56 Fed. Reg. 45584 (Sept. 6, 1991).

[6] 56 Fed. Reg. 8579 (Feb. 28, 1991).

[7] S.Rep. No. 116, 101st Cong., 1st Sess. 24-44 (1989).

individual; (B) a record of such an impairment; or (C) being regarded as having such an impairment."[8]

The core requirement of title I of the ADA is that no covered entity shall discriminate against a qualified individual with a disability because of the disability in regard to job application procedures, the hiring, advancement, or discharge of employees, employee compensation, job training, and other terms, conditions and privileges of employment. The term employer is defined as a person engaged in an industry affecting commerce who has 15 or more employees; however, for the two years following the effective date of the title, an employer means a person engaged in an industry affecting commerce who has 25 or more employees. The term qualified individual with a disability is defined as "an individual with a disability who, with or without reasonable accommodation, can perform the essential functions of the employment position that the person holds or desires."[9] These requirements also echo those in the section 504 regulations, particularly with regard to the requirement to provide reasonable accommodation unless such accommodation would pose an undue hardship on the operation of the business. The ADA specifically lists some defenses to a charge of discrimination including (1) that the alleged application of qualification standards has been shown to be job related and consistent with business necessity and such performance cannot be accomplished by reasonable accommodation, (2) the term qualification standards can include a requirement that an individual shall not pose a direct threat to the health or safety of other individuals in the work place, and (3) religious entities may give a preference in employment to individuals of a particular religion to perform work connected with carrying on the entities' activities.[10]

Major Issues Raised by the EEOC's ADA Regulations

The EEOC's ADA regulations closely parallel the statutory language of the ADA, its legislative history, and regulatory and judicial interpretation of section 504 of the Rehabilitation Act. However, certain additions have been made, such as definitions for the terms "substantially limits," "essential

---

[8] 29 U.S.C. sec. 706(8); ADA sec. 3, 42 U.S.C. sec. 12102(2).

[9] ADA, sec. 101(8), 42 U.S.C. sec. 12111.

[10] For a more detailed discussion of the statutory requirements of the ADA see "The Americans with Disabilities Act: An Overview of Major Provisions," CRS Rep. No. 90-366A (July 31, 1990).

functions," and "reasonable accommodation." An appendix is also included at the end of the regulations which provides further interpretation. In addition, the Commission has stated it will provide more detailed guidance in a compliance manual which is expected to be issued in February 1992. The Commission has indicated that the compliance manual will contain guidance on issues such as theories of discrimination, definitions of disability and of qualified individual with a disability, and reasonable accommodation and undue hardship, including the scope of reassignment and pre-employment inquiries.[11]

Specificity

One of the most common criticisms of the EEOC regulations is that they do not specifically delineate the exact requirements placed on employers. One commentator has observed: "[b]oth employers and the disabled are likely to be disappointed by the final regulations. They fail to provide specific rules or guidance on many key issues, opting instead for determinations to be made on a 'case by case basis.'"[12] This is clearly an intentional decision by the EEOC. In its appendix to its regulations, the EEOC states that "the ADA seeks to ensure access to equal employment opportunities based on merit... [it] thus establishes a process in which the employer must assess a disabled individual's ability to perform the essential functions of the specific job held or desired .... However, where that individual [with disabilities] functional limitation impedes such job performance, an employer must take steps to reasonably accommodate, and thus help overcome the particular impediment, unless to do so would impose an undue hardship. This process of identifying whether, and to what extent, a reasonable accommodation is required should be flexible and involve both the employer and the individual with disability. Of course, the determination of whether an individual is qualified for a particular position must necessarily be made on a case-by-case basis."[13] The EEOC further emphasized: "[t]his case-by-case approach is essential if qualified individuals of varying abilities are to receive equal opportunities to compete for an infinitely diverse range of jobs. For this reason, neither the ADA nor this part can supply the 'correct' answer in advance for each employment

---

[11] 56 Fed. Reg. 35726 (July 26, 1991).

[12] Shaller and Rosen, "A Guide to the EEOC's Final Regulations on the Americans with Disabilities Act," 17 Employee Relations L. J. 405 (1991-1992).

[13] 56 Fed. Reg. 35739 (July 26, 1991).

decision concerning an individual with a disability. Instead, the ADA simply establishes parameters to guide employers in how to consider, and take into account, the disabling condition involved."[14]

This case by case balancing approach taken by EEOC is the same as that taken under section 504 of the Rehabilitation Act. The Supreme Court in *Alexander v. Choate,* 469 U.S. 287 (1985), found that section 504 struck "a balance between the statutory rights of the handicapped to be integrated into society and the legitimate interests of federal grantees in preserving the integrity of their programs: while a grantee need not be required to make 'fundamental' or 'substantial' modifications to accommodate the handicapped, it may be required to make 'reasonable' ones." Such decisions are to be made on a case-by-case basis.

Definition of Individual with Disabilities

The issues revolving around the definition of individual with disabilities are among the most critical. The specific areas which may be of concern in this regard include the regulatory guidance on factors to be considered concerning whether an individual is substantially limited in a major life activity. These factors include "the duration or expected duration of the impairment." This raises the issue of whether temporary disabilities such as a broken leg would be covered. In the appendix to the regulation, the EEOC states that a broken leg that takes eight weeks to heal is an impairment of a fairly brief duration but does not indicate that this would be an automatic exclusion although it does note that "temporary, non-chronic impairments of short duration, with little or no long term or permanent impact are usually not disabilities."[15] The EEOC emphasizes that "the determination of whether an individual is substantially limited in a major life activity must be made on a case-by-case basis."[16] Similarly, the EEOC regulations do not directly address the controversial issue of whether obesity is a disability but note in the appendix that "except in rare circumstances, obesity is not considered a disabling impairment."[17]

Another aspect of the definition of individual with disabilities which has been controversial is that concerning the employment of former drug addicts. The ADA specifically provides that the term individual with a disability

---

[14] *Id.* at 35740.
[15] 56 Fed. Reg. 35741 (July 26, 1991).
[16] *Id.*
[17] *Id.*

"does not include an individual who is currently engaging in the illegal use of drugs, when the covered entity acts on the basis of such use."[18] However, the ADA definition does not exclude individuals who are no longer engaging in such activity. This has given rise to questions concerning whether certain employers, particularly law enforcement agencies, can take a previous history of drug abuse into account. This issue is not directly addressed in the EEOC regulations but is discussed in the appendix to the regulations. "An employer, such as a law enforcement agency, may also be able to impose a qualification standard that excludes individuals with a history of illegal use of drugs if it can show that the standard is job-related and consistent with business necessity."[19]

It should be noted that the EEOC definition of individual with disabilities is taken from the functional definition provided in the statute and does not list specific conditions. Although AIDS and HIV infection are not specifically mentioned in the act, the prior interpretation of section 504 and the legislative history of the ADA indicate that such coverage is intended.[20]

Definition of Direct Threat

One of the more controversial aspects of the EEOC regulations is the definition of "direct threat." The ADA defines the term "qualifications standards" so as to allow inclusion of a requirement that an individual not pose "a direct threat to the health or safety of other individuals in the workplace."[21] The EEOC regulations define the term direct threat as meaning "a significant risk of substantial harm to the health or safety of *the individual* or others that cannot be eliminated or reduced by reasonable accommodation."[22] The appendix elaborates on this. "If performing the particular functions of a job would result in a high probability of substantial harm to the individual, the employer could reject or discharge the individual unless a reasonable accommodation that would not cause an undue hardship would avert the harm. For example, an employer would not be required to hire an individual, disabled by narcolepsy, who frequently and unexpectedly loses consciousness for a carpentry job the essential functions of which require the use of power saws and other dangerous equipment, where no

---

[18] ADA, sec. 510, 42 U.S.C. sec. 12210.
[19] 56 Fed. Reg. 35746 (July 26, 1991).
[20] See e.g., S. Rep. No. 116, 101st Cong., 1st Sess. (1989).
[21] ADA sec. 103, 42 U.S.C. sec. 12113.
[22] 29 C.F.R. §1630.2(r) 56 Fed. Reg. 35736 (July 26, 1991) (emphasis added).

accommodation exists that will reduce or eliminate the risk."[23] However, the legislative history of the ADA refers only to a direct threat to others although the case law under section 504 is more ambiguous.[24]

Collective Bargaining Agreements

When an individual with disabilities applies for employment, he or she must be able to perform the essential functions of the position, with or without reasonable accommodation, in order to be otherwise qualified for the job. The EEOC regulations provide guidance on what these essential functions are and list certain factors which may be considered in determining whether a particular function is essential. These factors include the terms of a collective bargaining agreement. In addition, in its interpretative guidance on undue hardship, the EEOC notes that the terms of a collective bargaining agreement may be relevant to determining whether an accommodation would pose an undue hardship on the operation of a covered entity's business.[25]

This regulatory guidance is significant since there is a possibility of conflict between the requirements of the ADA and the provisions of collective bargaining agreements. For example, the ADA requires that an individual with disabilities be able to perform the essential functions of a job with or without reasonable accommodation and that this does not impose an undue hardship on the employer. Reasonable accommodation may necessitate a change in work hours; for example, a day-time shift. However, collective bargaining agreements not infrequently provide that the more desirable day-time shifts are to be made available on the basis of seniority. The issue posed is whether this conflict would result an undue hardship, thus not requiring the employer to make the accommodation.

By adding collective bargaining agreements to the factors that may be considered in determining whether a particular function is essential and by providing some possibility that conflicts with such agreements may give rise to an "undue hardship," the EEOC provides some guidance but still leaves considerable uncertainty as to the exact interplay between the ADA and

---

[23] 56 Fed. Reg. 35745 (July 26, 1991).

[24] See *Davis v. Meese*, 692 F. Supp. 505 (E.D.Pa 1988), *aff'd without opinion*, 895 F.2d 592 (3d Cir. 1989), where an insulin dependent diabetic was denied employment as an investigative specialist and special agent with the FBI due to a "very real danger of serious harm to the special agent or investigative specialist and uninvolved third parties, as well as potential serious harm and disruption to the operation of the FBI..." At 520.

[25] 56 Fed. Reg. 35752 (July 26, 1991).

collective bargaining agreements. The EEOC recognized that its guidance was not comprehensive and stated: "These highly complex issues require extensive research and analysis and warrant further consideration. Accordingly, the Commission has decided to address the issues in depth in future Compliance Manual sections and policy guidances."[26]

Insurance

Issues involving the provision of insurance benefits to individual with disabilities have been some of the most difficult under the ADA. The ADA contains a specific exemption relating to insurance: "Title I through IV of this Act shall not be construed to prohibit or restrict – (1) an insurer, hospital or medical service company, health maintenance organization, or any agent, or entity that administers benefit plans, or similar organizations from underwriting risks, classifying risks, or administering such risks that are based on or not inconsistent with State law; or (2) a person or organization covered by this Act from establishing, sponsoring, observing or administering the terms of a bona fide benefit plan that are based on underwriting risks, classifying risks, or administering such risks that are based on or not inconsistent with State law; or (3) a person or organization covered by this Act from establishing, sponsoring, observing or administering the terms of a bona fide benefit plan that is not subject to State laws that regulate insurance. Paragraphs (1), (2) and (3) shall not be used as a subterfuge to evade the purposes of title I and III."[27] These requirements are incorporated virtually verbatim in the EEOC regulations.[28]

The EEOC regulatory appendix provides some clarification of this language. It indicates that an employer's activities regarding insurance may not violate the ADA even if they result in limitations on the individual with disabilities as long as there is no subterfuge. The determination of subterfuge is not dependent on the date the insurance or employee benefit plan was adopted. However, the EEOC indicates that an employer cannot deny a qualified individual with a disability equal access to insurance or subject an qualified individual with a disability to different terms and conditions based solely on the disability assuming that the disability does not pose increased risks.[29]

---

[26] 56 Fed. Reg. 35727 (July 26, 1991).
[27] 42 U.S.C. §12201(c).
[28] 56 Fed. Reg. 35739 (July 26, 1991); 29 C.F.R. §1630.16(f).
[29] 56 Fed. Reg. 35753 (July 26, 1991).

The EEOC guidance on the subject of insurance is sparse and leaves open numerous issues such as whether an employer should consider the effects that changes in insurance coverage will have on individuals with disabilities before making those changes. For example, regulatory guidance could be of significant assistance in determining whether employers can change their health insurance coverage to limit coverage on certain conditions. Recently the fifth circuit court of appeals in *McGann v. H. & H Music Company,* No. 90-2672, 1991 U.S. App. LEXIS 26056 (5th Cir. Nov. 4, 1991), affirmed the district court decision that under provisions of the Employee Retirement Income Security Act of 1974 (ERISA), 29 U.S.C. §§1001-1461, an employer "has an absolute right to alter the terms of medical coverage available to plan beneficiaries." In *McGann,* the plaintiff was covered under a policy which provided for lifetime medical benefits of up to $1,000,000 for all employees. When the plaintiff discovered he was HIV infected, he filed claims with the plan for his medical bills and discussed his condition with his employers. Shortly thereafter, the employer made changes in its medical coverage including a limitation of benefits payable for AIDS-related claims to a maximum of $5,000. No limitation was placed on any other catastrophic illness. The employer's motive was described by the court as to ensure the future existence of the plan and not specifically to retaliate against the employee.

McGann involved an ERISA provision prohibiting the discharge of or discrimination against a participant for exercising any rights to which he was entitled to under the provisions of an employee benefit plan.[30] No claims were made under section 504 of the Rehabilitation Act (prohibiting discrimination against individuals with disabilities in any program or activity receiving federal financial assistance) and the ADA provisions relating to employment will not be effective until July 26, 1992. The issue which *McGann* poses in this context is whether, after the effective date of the ADA provisions, actions like that of the employer would violate the ADA. It could be argued that they would not be violative in that general limitations on coverage for particular conditions, such as limitations on the days of inpatient hospital care, are permissible even if they have a disparate impact on individuals with disabilities.[31] This argument could further be supported by nothing that under section 504 of the Rehabilitation Act, the third circuit

---

[30] 29 U.S.C. §1140.

[31] See *Alexander v. Choate,* 469 U.S. 287 (1985), where the Supreme Court upheld under §504 a state limitation on the number of annual impatient hospital days that state Medicaid would pay hospitals on behalf of a Medicaid patient.

had found that limitations on covered private inpatient psychiatric care were permissible even though no such limits were set on physical disabilities.[32]

The Senate Report on the ADA could also be cited to support this conclusion. It notes that "[u]nder the ADA, a person with a disability cannot be denied insurance or be subject to different terms or conditions of insurance based on disability alone, *if the disability does no pose increased risks* .... Without such a clarification, this legislation could arguably find violative of its provisions any action taken by an insurer or employer which treats disabled persons differently under an insurance or benefit plan because they represent an increased hazard of death or illness."[33] IN *McGann,* the court had noted that the business had limited coverage of AIDS in an attempt to preserve its plan and its action was not directed at the plaintiff as an individual. It could be argued, then, that the ADA would not be violated by such an action since the ADA would allow distinctions based on different risks of death or illness.

However, an argument also cold be made that the factual pattern presented by *McGann* would be violative of the ADA. In *McGann,* no limitation on other catastrophic diseases or conditions was made; HIV infection was singed out for limitation. It could be argued that although the ADA may allow limits on insurance where there are different hazards of death or illness, it does not allow discrimination among different types of conditions which have similar risks.

McGann illustrates one type of issue which may arise concerning insurance. Issues relating to risk assessment and classifications and the relationship between risk and cost as well as others will undoubtedly be presented. Also key to the determination of all these issues may be how "subterfuge" is applied. The EEOC noted in its comments to its final rules that commentators had "presented a wide range of opinions on insurance-related-matters, and the Commission will consider the comments as it continues to analyze these complex matters."[34]

Worker's Compensation

The ADA makes it unlawful for an entity to conduct a medical examination of a prospective applicant for employment or of an employee or

---

[32] *Doe v. Colautti,* 592 F.2d 704 (3d Cir. 1979), cited with approval in *Alexander v. Choate,* 469 U.S. 287 (1985).

[33] S. Rep. 116, 101st Cong., 1st Sess. 182-183 (1989).

[34] 56 Fed. Reg. 35726 (July 26, 1991).

to make inquiries regarding whether the applicant or employee has a disability or the severity of the disability except under certain specified conditions.[35] There was some ambiguity under the proposed EEOC regulations concerning whether the ADA allowed inquiries concerning an applicant's or employee's worker's compensation. In its interpretative guidance the EEOC indicates that an employer cannot "inquire at the pre-offer stage about an applicant's worker's compensation history."[36] However, the guidance also notes that "[s]tate worker's compensation laws are not preempted by the ADA.... These laws require the collection of information from individuals for state administrative purposes that do not conflict with the ADA.... Consequently, employers or other covered entities may submit information to state worker's compensation offices or second injury funds in accordance with state worker's compensation laws without violating this part."[37] The EEOC also noted that it will discuss other workers' compensation issues in future policy guidance statements.[38]

CONCLUSION

The Equal Employment Opportunities Commission (EEOC) has recently promulgated final regulations under title I of the Americans with Disabilities Act, which prohibits discrimination against individuals with disabilities. With regard to employment, the ADA essentially provides that no covered entity shall discriminate against a qualified individual with a disability because of the disability in regard to job application procedures, the hiring, advancement, or discharge of employees, employee compensation, job training and other terms, conditions and privileges of employment. Title I of the ADA and the EEOC regulations will go into effect for employers who employ more than 25 employees on July 26, 1992. For employers who employ 15 or more employees, the effective date will be July 26, 1994.

The EEOC's ADA regulations closely parallel the statutory language of the ADA, its legislative history, and regulatory and judicial interpretation of section 504 of the Rehabilitation Act of 1973. The regulations do provide more detailed guidance in certain areas, for example with the definition of "essential functions," the definition of individual with disabilities, and the

---

[35] 42 U.S.C. §12112(c)(2).

[36] 56 Fed. Reg. 35750 (July 26, 1991).

[37] 56 Fed. Reg. 35751 (July 26, 1991).

[38] 56 Fed. Reg. 35727 (July 26, 1991).

definition of direct threat. However, the regulations have been criticized as failing to provide sufficient specific guidance in other areas. This issue has been raised generally concerning the case-by-case approach delineated in the regulations and more specifically regarding issues raised by collective bargaining agreements, insurance, and worker's compensation. EEOC has noted that it will issue a compliance manual in February 1992 which may address some of these issues.

Chapter 6

The Americans with Disabilities Act (ADA): An Overview of the Major Provisions and Issues

Nancy Lee Jones

Introduction

The Americans with Disabilities Act (ADA), enacted on July 16, 1990, provides broad nondiscrimination protection for individuals with disabilities in employment, public services, public accommodations and services operated by public entities, transportation, and telecommunications.

Background

The Americans with Disabilities Act, ADA, P.L. 101-336, has often been described as the most sweeping nondiscrimination legislation since the Civil Rights Act of 1964. It provides broad nondiscrimination protection for individuals with disabilities in employment, public services, public accommodation and services operated by private entities, transportation, and telecommunications. As stated in the Act, its purpose is "to provide a clear and comprehensive national mandate for the elimination of discrimination against individuals with disabilities."[1] Enacted on July 26, 1990, the majority of the ADA's provisions took effect 1992. Although the ADA is still in the early developing years for civil rights jurisprudence, several major issues have surfaced. These include questions concerning what constitutes a disability, and what is a "reasonable accommodation." This chapter will briefly examine the major provisions of the ADA and selected issues that have arisen under the Act.

Prior to this examination, it would be helpful to note the historical antecedents of the ADA. An existing federal statutory provision, section 504 of the Rehabilitation Act of 1973, 29 U.S.C. § 794, prohibits discrimination against an otherwise qualified individual with a disability, solely on the basis of the disability, in any program or activity that received federal financial assistance, the executive agencies or the U.S. Postal Service.[2] Many of the concepts used in the ADA originated in section 504 and its interpretations; however, there is one major difference: while section 504's prohibition against discrimination is tied to the receipt of federal financial assistance, the ADA also covers entities not receiving such funds. The ADA contains a specific provision stating that except as otherwise provided in the Act, nothing in the Act shall be construed to apply a lesser standard than the standards applied under title V of the Rehabilitation Act (which includes section 504) or the regulations issued by federal agencies pursuant to such title.[3]

DEFINITION OF DISABILITY

The definitions in the ADA, particularly the definition of "disability", are the starting point for an analysis of rights provided by the law. The term "disability", with respect to an individual, is defined as "(A) a physical or mental impairment that substantially limits one or more of the major life activities of such individual; (B) a record of such an impairment; or (C) being regarded as having such an impairment."[4] This definition, which has been the subject of numerous cases brought under the ADA, is drawn from the definitional section applicable to section 504.[5]

---

[1] 42 U.S.C. § 12101(b)(1).
[2] 29 U.S.C. § 794.
[3] 42 U.S.C. § 12201(a).
[4] 42 U.S.C. § 12102(2).
[5] 29 U.S.C. § 706(8).

The definition of "disability" was further elaborated in title V of the ADA. Section 510 provides that the term "individual with a disability" in the ADA does not include an individual who is currently engaging in the illegal use of drugs when the covered entity acts on the basis of such use.[6] An individual who has been rehabilitated would be covered. However, the conference report language clarifies that the provision does not permit individuals to invoke coverage simply by showing they are participating in a drug rehabilitation program; they must refrain from using drugs.[7] The conference report also indicates that the limitation in coverage is not intended to be narrowly construed to only persons who use drugs "on the day of, or within a matter of weeks before, the action in question."[8] The definitional section of the Rehabilitation Act that applies to section 504 was also amended to create uniformity with this definition.

Section 508 provides that an individual shall not be considered to have a disability solely because that individual is a transvestite.[9] Section 511 similarly provides that homosexuality and bisexuality are not disabilities under the Act and that the term disability does not include transvestism, transsexualism, pedophilia, exhibitionism, voyeurism, gender identity disorders not resulting from physical impairment, or other sexual behavior disorders, compulsive gambling, kleptomania, or pyromania, or psychoactive substance use disorders resulting from current illegal use of drugs.[10]

The issues involving the definition of "disability" have been among the most controversial under the ADA. The Equal Employment Opportunity Commission (EEOC) issued detailed guidance on the definition on March 15, 1995. The EEOC found that the following conditions would not constitute impairments: environmental, cultural, and economic disadvantages; age; pregnancy; common personality traits; and normal deviations in height, weight and strength. However, certain aspects of these conditions could give rise to an impairment. For example, complications arising from pregnancy or conditions associated with age, such as hearing loss, could be considered to be disabilities. The guidance also include the EEOC's interpretation of the third prong of the definition – "regarded as having disability." This category was seen by EEOC as including individuals

---

[6] 42 U.S.C. § 12210.

[7] H.Conf.Rep.No. 101-596, 101st Cong, 2d Sess. 64; 1990 U.S. Code Cong. & Admin. News 573.

[8] *Id.*

[9] 42 U.S.C. § 12208.

[10] 42 U.S.C. § 12211.

who are subjected to discrimination on the basis of genetic information relating to illness, disease or other disorders.[11]

Cases brought concerning the definition of "disability" under the ADA have included questions on obesity,[12] cancer,[13] HIV infection,[14] and infertility.[15] In addition, a recent case found that, contrary to EEOC guidance, a disability that can be controlled by medications was not to be considered a disability under the ADA.[16] Although a detailed analysis of these cases is beyond the scope of this chapter, two general observations may be made. First, any argument that attempts to make a blanket determination that all individuals with a particular disability are covered is viewed with suspicion by the courts and will often fail. Second, the interpretation of the ADA is still evolving. The courts are not in agreement on a number of these questions, and they do not always agree with the interpretation advanced by the EEOC.

---

[11] *EEOC Compliance Manual,* Section 902; *BNA's Americans with Disabilities Act Manual* 70:1131. The issue of coverage of genetic disorders has been widely discussed. See Jones, "Genetic Information: Discrimination and Privacy Issues," CRS Rep. No. 96-808 A.

[12] The EEOC's ADA regulations state that absent unusual circumstances, "obesity is not considered a disabling impairment." 29 C.F.R. § 1630.2(j)(Appendix). However, several cases have found situations where obesity might be covered. See, e.g., *Cook v. Rhode Island,* 10 F.3d 17 (1st Cir. 1993), and *EEOC v. Texas Bus Lines,* 923 F.Supp. 878 (S.D.Tex. 1996).

[13] In most cases, an individual with cancer would most likely be covered by the ADA, since the cancer would probably limit a major life activity. But the fifth circuit court of appeals held that a woman who received radiation treatments for breast cancer was not covered, since she missed very few days of work and was therefore not limited in a major life activity. *Ellison v. Software Spectrum, Inc.,* 85 F.3d 187 (5th Cir. 1996).

[14] The majority of cases have following the lead of the EEOC, which has found that HIV infection is "inherently substantially limiting." [29 C.F.R. § 1630.2(j)(Appendix)]. However, see *Ennis v. National Association of Business and Educational Radio,* 53 F. 3d 55 (4th Cir. 1995), where the court found that a child who was HIV-infected but asymptomatic did not have a disability for ADA purposes.

[15] A recent court of appeals case found that infertility is not a disability because the ability to reproduce in not a major life activity. *Krauel v. Iowa Methodist Medical Center,* 95 F.3d 674 (8th Cir. 1996). However, cases at the district court level are split. See, e.g., *Pacourck v. Inland Steel Co.,* 916 F. Supp. 797 (N.D. Ill 1996), where the court found that reproduction was a major life activity; *Krauel v. Iowa Methodist Medical Center,* 915 F.Supp. 102 (S.D. Iowa 1995), *aff'd,* 95 F.3d 674 (8th Cir. 1996), where the court found that reproduction is a "lifestyle choice" and not a major life activity.

[16] *Murphy v. United Parcel Service,* 1996 U.S.Dist LEXIS 17619 (D.Kan. 1996).

EMPLOYMENT

General Requirements

Title I of the ADA provides that no covered entity shall discriminate against a qualified individual with a disability because of the disability in regard to job application procedures, the hiring, advancement, or discharge of employees, employee compensation, job training, and other terms, conditions, and privileges of employment.[17] The term employer is defined as a person engaged in an industry affecting commerce who has 15 or more employees.[18] Therefore, the employment section of the ADA, unlike the section on public accommodations, which will be discussed subsequently, is limited in scope to employers with 15 or more employees. This parallels the coverage provided in the Civil Right Act of 1964.

The term "employee" with respect to employment in a foreign country includes an individual who is a citizen of the United States; however, it is not unlawful for a covered entity to take action that constitutes discrimination with respect to an employee in a workplace in a foreign country if compliance would cause the covered entity to violate the law of the foreign country.[19]

If the issue raised under the ADA is employment related, and the threshold issues of meeting the definition of and individual with a disability and involving an employer employing over fifteen individuals are met, the next step is to determine whether the individual is a qualified individual with a disability who, with or without reasonable accommodation, can perform the essential functions of the job.

Title I defines a "qualified individual with a disability." Such an individual is "an individual with a disability who, with or without reasonable accommodation, can perform the essential functions of the employment positions that such person holds or desires."[20] The ADA incorporates many of the concepts set forth in the regulations promulgated pursuant to section 504, including the requirement to provide reasonable accommodation unless

---

[17] 42 U.S.C. § 12112(a).

[18] 42 U.S.C. § 12111(5).

[19] P.L. 102-166 added this provision.

[20] 42 U.S.C. § 12111(8). The EEOC has stated that a function may be essential because (1) the position exists to perform the duty, (2) there are a limited number of employees available who could perform the function, or (3) the function is highly specialized. 29 C.F.R. § 1630(n) (2). A number of issues have been litigated concerning essential functions. For example, most courts have found that regular attendance is an essential function of most jobs. See, e.g., *Carr v. Reno*, 23 F.3d 525 (D.C. Cir. 1994).

such accommodation would pose an undue hardship on the operation of the business.[21]

"Reasonable accommodation" is defined in the ADA as including making existing facilities readily accessible to and usable by individuals with disabilities, and job, restructuring, part-time or modified work schedules, reassignment to a vacant position, acquisition or modification of equipment or devices, adjustment of examinations or training materials or policies, provision of qualified readers or interpreters or other similar accommodations.[22] "Undue hardship" is defined as "an action requiring significant difficulty or expense."[23]

The concepts of reasonable accommodation and undue hardship were discussed by the seventh circuit in *Vande Zande v. State of Wisconsin Department of Administration.*[24] In *Vande Zande* the court found that the cost of the accommodation cannot be disproportionate to the benefit. "Even if an employer is so large or wealthy – or, like the principal defendant in this case, is a state, which can raise taxes in order to finance any accommodations that it must make to disabled employees – that it may not be able to plead 'undue hardship', it would not be required to expend enormous sums in order to bring about a trivial improvement in the life of a disabled employee."[25]

Another issue that has arisen is the interplay between rights under the ADA for reasonable accommodation and collective bargaining agreements. In a recent seventh circuit court of appeals decision, the court found that "the ADA does not require disabled individuals to be accommodated by sacrificing the collectively bargained, bona fide seniority rights of other employees."[26] This decision was contrary to arguments which had been advanced by the EEOC. The EEOC had argued that although the EEOC does not require displacement of another employee to accommodate an individual with a disability, employers and unions have a responsibility to negotiate in good faith a variance from the collective bargaining agreement.

---

[21] See 45 C.F.R. Part 84.

[22] 42 U.S.C. § 12111(9).

[23] 42 U.S.C. § 12111(10). The definition also provides various factors to be considered in determining whether an action would create an undue hardship. These include the nature and cost of the accommodation, the overall financial resources of the facility, the overall financial resources of the covered entity, and the type of operation or operations of the covered entity.

[24] 44 F.3d 538 (7th Cir. 1995).

[25] *Id.* at 542-543. See also *Schmidt v. Methodist Hospital of Indiana*, 89 F.3d 342 (7th Cir. 1996), where the court found that reasonable accommodation does not require an employer to provide everything an employee requests.

[26] *Eckles v. Consolidated Rail Corporation*, 94 F.3d 1041, 1051 (7th Cir. 1996).

Employment Inquiries Relating to Disability

Before an offer of employment is made, an employer may not ask a disability related question or require a medical examination.[27] The EEOC in its guidance on this issue stated that the rationale for this exclusion was to isolate an employer's consideration of an applicant's non-medical qualifications from any consideration of the applicant's medical condition.[28] However, once an offer is made disability related questions and medical examinations are permitted as long as all individuals who have been offered a job in that category are asked the same questions and given the same examinations.[29]

Defenses to a Charge of Discrimination

The ADA specifically lists some defenses to a charge of discrimination, including (1) that the alleged application of qualification standards has been shown to be job related and consistent with business necessity and such performance cannot be accomplished by reasonable accommodation, (2) the term "qualification standards" can include a requirement that an individual shall not pose a direct threat to the health or safety of other individuals in the workplace,[30] and (3) religious entities may give a preference in employment to individuals of a particular religion to perform work connected with carrying on the entities' activities.[31] In addition, religious entities may require that all applicants and employees conform to the religious tenets of the organization. The Secretary of Health and Human Services has, pursuant to a statutory requirement, listed infectious and communicable diseases transmitted through the handling of food and if the risk cannot be eliminated by reasonable accommodation, a covered entity may refuse to assign or continue to assign an individual with such a disease to a job involving food handling.

---

[27] 42 U.S.C. § 12112.
[28] EEOC, "ADA Enforcement Guidance: Preemployment Disability-Related Questions and Medical Examinations," Oct. 10, 1995.
[29] *Id.*
[30] The EEOC in its regulations states that the following factors should be considered when determining whether an individual poses a direct threat: the duration of the risk, the nature and severity of the potential harm, the likelihood that the potential harm will occur and the imminence of the potential harm. 29 C.F.R. § 1630.2(r).
[31] 42 U.S.C. § 12113.

Drug Addicts and Alcoholics

A controversial issue that arose during the enactment of the ADA regarding employment concerned the application of the Act to drug addict and alcoholics. The ADA provides that, with regard to employment, *current* illegal drug users are not considered to be qualified individuals with disabilities. However, former drug users and alcoholics would be covered by the Act if they are able to perform the essential functions of the job. In the appendix to its regulations, EEOC further notes that "an employer, such as a law enforcement agency, may also be able to impose a qualification standard that excludes individuals with a history of illegal use of drugs if it can show that the standard is job-related and consistent with business necessity."[32] Title I also provides that a covered entity may prohibit the illegal use of drugs and the use alcohol at the workplace.[33]

Remedies

The remedies and procedures set forth in sections 705, 706, 707, 709, and 710 of the Civil Rights Act of 1964,[34] are incorporated by reference. This provides for certain administrative enforcement as well as allowing for individual suits. The Civil Rights Act of 1991, P.L. 102-166, expanded the remedies of injunctive relief and back pay.[35] A plaintiff who was the subject of unlawful intentional discrimination (as opposed to an employment practice that is discriminatory because of its disparate impact) may recover compensatory and punitive damages. In order to receive punitive damages, the plaintiff must show that there was a discriminatory practice engaged in with malice or with reckless indifference to the rights of the aggrieved individual. The amount that can be awarded in punitive and compensatory damages is capped, with the amounts varying from $50,000 to $300,000 depending upon the size of the business. Similarly, there is also a "good faith" exception to the award of damages with regard to reasonable accommodation.

---

[32] 29 C.F.R. Appendix §1630.3.

[33] 42 U.S.C. § 12114(c); 29 C.F.R. § 1630.16(b)(4).

[34] 42 U.S.C. §§ 2000e-4, 2000e-5, 2000e-6, 2000e-7.

[35] For a detailed discussion of this Act see "The Civil Rights Act of 1991: A Legal History and Analysis," CRS Rep. 92-85A (Jan. 10, 1992).

PUBLIC SERVICES

Title II of the ADA provides that no qualified individual with a disability shall be excluded from participation on or be denied the benefits of the services, programs, or activities of public entity or be subjected to discrimination by any such entity.[36] "Public entity" is defined as state and local governments, any department or other instrumentality of a state and local governments, any department or other instrumentality of a state or local government, and certain transportation authorities. The ADA does not apply to the executive branch of the Federal Government; the executive branch is covered by section 504 of the Rehabilitation Act of 1973.[37]

The Department of Justice regulations for title II contain a specific section on program accessibility. Each service, program, or activity conducted by a public entity, when viewed in its entirety, must be readily accessible to and usable by individuals with disabilities. However, a public entity is not required to make each of its existing facilities accessible.[38] Program accessibility is limited in certain situations involving historic preservation. In addition, in meeting the program accessibility requirement, a public entity is not required to take any action that would result in a fundamental alteration in the nature of its service, program, or activity or in undue financial and administrative burdens.[39]

Although title II has not been the subject of as much litigation as title I, several issues have been raised. For example, a Hawaii regulation requiring the quarantine of all dogs, including guide dogs for visually impaired individuals, was found to violate title II.[40] Cases have also arisen concerning the extent to which title II requires state examiners to modify their exam procedures for individuals with disabilities;[41] when curb ramps are

---

[36] 42 U.S.C. §§ 12131-12133.

[37] 29 U.S.C. § 794.

[38] 28 C.F.R. §35.150.

[39] *Id.*

[40] *Crowder v. Kitagawa,* 81 F.3d 1480, 1484 (9th Cir. 1996). The court stated: "Although Hawaii's quarantine requirements applies equally to all persons entering the state with a dog, its enforcement burdens visually-impaired persons in a manner different and greater than it burdens others. Because of the unique dependence upon guide dogs among many of the visually-impaired, Hawaii's quarantine effectively denies these persons... meaningful access to state services, programs, and activities while such services, programs, and activities remain open and easily accessible by others."

[41] This has most commonly arisen concerning bar exams. See *D'Amico v. New York State Board of Law Examiners,* 813 F.Supp. 217 (W.D.N.Y. 1993), where the court ordered that a visually impaired individual be allowed to take the bar exam over a four day, rather than a two day, time period.

required;[42] the application of title II to a city ordinance allowing open burning;[43] the application of title II to prisoners;[44] and discrimination among individuals with disabilities.[45]

This title also provides specific requirements for public transportation by intercity and commuter rail and for public transportation other than by aircraft or certain rail operations.[46] All new vehicles purchased or leased by a public entity that operates a fixed route system must be accessible, and good faith efforts must be demonstrated with regard to the purchase or lease of accessible used vehicles. Retrofitting of existing buses is not required. Paratransit services must be provided by a public entity that operates a fixed route service, other than one providing solely commuter bus service.[47] Rail systems must have at least one car per train that is accessible to individuals with disabilities.[48]

The enforcement remedies of section 505 of the Rehabilitation Act of 1973, 29[49] U.S.C. § 794a, are incorporated by reference. These remedies are similar to those of title VI of the Civil Rights Act of 1964, and include damages and injunctive relief. The Attorney General has promulgated regulations relating to subpart A of the title,[50] and the Secretary of Transportation has issued regulations regarding transportation.[51]

PUBLIC ACCOMMODATIONS

Title III provides that no individual shall be discriminated against on the basis of disability in the full and equal enjoyment of the goods, services, facilities, privileges, advantages, or accommodations of any place of public

---

[42] In *Kinney v. Yerusalim,* 812 F.Supp. 547 (E.D. Pa. 1993), *aff'd* 9 F.3d 1067 (3d Cir. 1993), *cert.den.* 114 S.Ct. 1545 (1994), the court found that street repair projects must include curb ramps for individuals with disabilities. See also 28 C.F.R. § 35.151(e)(1), where the Department of Justice detailed the requirements for curb ramps.

[43] *Heather K. v. City of Mallard, Iowa, 1996 WL 683587 (N.D.Iowa).*

[44] There is currently a split concerning whether the ADA applies to state prisons. A California district court has held that state prisons are covered. *Armstrong v. Wilson,* 942 F.Supp. 1252 (N.D. Calif. 1996). On the other hand, the fourth circuit had held that the ADA does not apply to prisons. *Torcasio v. Murray,* 57 F. 3d 1340 (4th Cir. 1995).

[45] In *Helen L. v. DiDario,* 46 F.3d 325 (3d Cir. 1995), *cert. denied,* 116 S.Ct. 64 (1995), the court found that title II would cover discrimination among individuals with disabilities.

[46] 42 U.S.C. §§ 12141-12165.

[47] 42 U.S.C. § 12143.

[48] 42 U.S.C. § 12162.

[49] 42 U.S.C. § 12133.

[50] 28 C.F.R. Part 35.

[51] 49 C.F.R. parts 27, 37, 38.

accommodation by any person who owns, leases (or leases to), or operates a place of public accommodation.[52] Entities that are covered by the term "public accommodation" are listed, and include, among other, hotels, restaurants, theaters, auditoriums, laundromats, museums, parks, zoos, private schools, day care centers, professional offices of health care providers, and gymnasiums.[53] Religious institutions or entities controlled by religious institutions are not included on the list.

There are some limitations on the nondiscrimination requirements, and a failure to remove architectural barriers is not a violation unless such a removal is "readily achievable."[54] "Readily achievable" is defined as meaning "easily accomplishable and able to be carried out without much difficulty or expense."[55] The nondiscrimination mandate also does not require that an entity permit an individual to participate in or benefit from the services of a public accommodation where such an individual poses a direct threat to the health or safety of others. Similarly, reasonable modifications in practices, policies or procedures are required unless they would fundamentally alter the nature of the goods, services, facilities, or privileges or they would result in an undue burden.[56] An under burden is defined as an action involving "significant difficulty or expense."[57]

Title III contains a specific exemption for religious entities.[58] This applies when an entity is controlled by a religious entity. For example, a preschool that is run by a religious entity would not be covered under the ADA; however, a preschool, that is not run by a religious entity but that rents space from the religious entity, would be covered by title III.

One of the issues that has arisen under title III is whether a place of public accommodation is limited to actual physical structures. The first Circuit Court of Appeals has held that public accommodations are not so limited reasoning that "to exclude this broad category of businesses from the reach of Title II and limit the application of Title III to physical structures which persons must enter to obtain goods and services would run afoul of the purpose of the ADA."[59] A related issues is whether franchisors are subject to title III. In *Nef v. American Dairy Queen Corp.,* the Fifth Circuit

---

[52] 42 U.S.C. § 12182.
[53] 42 U.S.C. § 12181.
[54] 42 U.S.C. § 12182(b)(2)(A)(iv).
[55] 42 U.S.C. § 12181.
[56] 42 U.S.C. § 12182(b)(2)(A).
[57] 28 C.F.R. § 36.104.
[58] 42 U.S.C. § 12187.
[59] *Carparts Distribution Center, Inc. v. Automotive Wholesaler's Association of New England, Inc.,* 37 F.3d. 12 (1st Cir. 1994).

Court of Appeals found that a franchisor with limited control over the store a franchisee runs is not covered under title III of the ADA.[60]

Title III also contains provisions relating to the prohibition of discrimination in public transportation services provided by private entities. Purchases of over-the-road buses are to be made in accordance with regulations issued by the Secretary of Transportation.[61]

The remedies and procedures of title II of the Civil Rights Act of 1964 are incorporated in Title III of the ADA. Title II of the Civil Rights Act has generally been interpreted to include injunctive relief, not damages. In addition, state and local governments can apply to the Attorney General to certify that state or local building codes meet or exceed the minimum accessibility requirements of the ADA. The Attorney General may bring pattern or practice suits with a maximum civil penalty of &50,000 for the first violation and $100,000 for a violation in a subsequent case. The monetary damages sought by the Attorney General do not include punitive damages. Courts may also consider an entity's "good faith" efforts in considering the amount of the civil penalty. Factors to be considered in determining good faith include whether an entity could have reasonably anticipated the need for an appropriate type of auxiliary aid to accommodate the unique needs of particular individual with a disability. Regulations relating to public accommodations have been promulgated by the Department of Justice[62] and regulations relating to the transportation provisions of title III have been promulgated by the Department of Transportation.[63]

TELECOMMUNICATIONS

Title IV of the ADA amends title II of the Communications Act of 1934[64] by adding a section providing that the Federal Communications Commission shall ensure that interstate and intrastate telecommunications relay services are available, to the extent possible and in the most efficient manner, to hearing-impaired and speech-impaired individuals. Any

---

[60] 58 F.3d 1063 (5th Cir. 1995).

[61] This section was amended by P.L. 104-59 to provide that accessibility requirements for private over-the-road buses must be met by small providers within three years after the issuance of final regulations and with respect to other providers, within two years after the issuance of such regulations.

[62] 28 C.F.R. Part 36.

[63] 49 C.F.R. Parts 27, 37, 38.

[64] 47 U.S.C. §§201 et seq.

television public service announcement that is produced or funded in whole or part by any agency or instrumentality of the federal governments shall include closed captioning of the verbal content of the announcement. The FCC is given enforcement authority with certain exceptions.[65]

MISCELLANEOUS PROVISIONS IN TITLE V

Title V contains an amalgam of provisions, several of which generated considerable controversy during ADA debate. Section 501 concerns the relationship of the ADA to other statutes and bodies of law. Subpart (a) states that "except as otherwise provided in this Act, nothing in the Act shall be construed to apply a lesser standard than the standards applied under title V of the Rehabilitation Act ... or the regulations issued by Federal agencies pursuant to such title." Subpart (b) provides that nothing in the Act shall be construed to invalidate or limit the remedies, rights and procedures of any federal, state or local law that provides greater or equal protection. Nothing in the Act is to be construed to preclude the prohibition of or restrictions on smoking. Subpart (d) provides that the Act does not require and individual with a disability to accept an accommodation which that individual chooses not to accept.[66]

Subpart (c) of section 501 limits the application of the Act with respect to the coverage of insurance; however, the subsection may not be used as a subterfuge to evade the purposes of titles I and III. The exact parameters of insurance coverage under the ADA are somewhat uncertain. As the EEOC has stated: "The interplay between the nondiscrimination principles of the ADA and employer provide health insurance, which is predicated on the ability to make health-related distinctions, is both unique and complex."[67] In a case that may have wide impact the Eighth Circuit Court of Appeals issued a preliminary injunction compelling the plaintiff employer to pay for chemotherapy that required an autologous bone marrow transplant. The plaintiff was diagnosed with an aggressive form of breast cancer and her oncologist recommended entry into a clinical trial program that randomly

---

[65] 47 U.S.C. §225.

[66] 29 U.S.C. §§790 *et seq.*

[67] EEOC: Interim Policy Guidance on ADA and Health Insurance, June 8, 1993. This guidance deals solely with the ADA implications of disability-based health insurance plan distinctions and states that "Insurance distinctions that are not based on disability, and that are applied equally to all insured employees, do not discriminate on the basis of disability and so do not violate the ADA." An example given of this permitted distinction was differences between the levels of coverage for physical and mental conditions.

assigns half of its participants to high dose chemotherapy that necessitates an autologous bone marrow transplant. Because of the possibility that the plaintiff might have the more expensive bone marrow treatment, the employer's health plan refused to precertify the placement noting that the policy covered high dose chemotherapy only for certain types of cancer, not breast cancer. The court concluded that, "if the evidence shows that a given treatment is non-experimental – that is, if it is widespread, safe, and a significant improvement on traditional therapies – and the plan provides the treatment for other conditions directly comparable to the one at issue, the denial of treatment violates the ADA."[68]

Another significant decision involving insurance coverage found that the plaintiff was entitled to have an opportunity to show that the distinction between mental and physical disabilities in long-term disability coverage is not justified by sound actuarial principles. Also of note with regard to this decision is that it was brought not under title I but under title III. The court found that "the statutory language of the Disabilities Act is sufficiently broad to prohibit discrimination in the contents of insurance products, not just physical access to insurance company offices."[69]

Section 502 abrogates the Eleventh Amendment state immunity from suit. Section 503 prohibits retaliation and coercion against an individual who has opposed an act or practice made unlawful by the ADA. Section 504 requires the Architectural and Transportation Barriers Compliance Board (ATBCB) to issue guidelines regarding accessibility. Section 505 provides for attorneys' fees in "any action or administrative proceeding" under the Act. Section 506 provides for technical assistance to help entities covered by the Act in understanding their responsibilities. Section 507 provides for a study by the National Council on Disability regarding wilderness designations and wilderness land management practices and "reaffirms" that nothing in the wilderness Act is to be construed as prohibiting the use of a wheelchair in a wilderness area by an individual whose disability requires the use of a wheelchair. Section 513 provides that "where appropriate and to the extent authorized by law, the use of alternative means of dispute resolution ... is encouraged...."[70] Section 514 provides for severability of any provision of the Act that is found to be unconstitutional.

The coverage of Congress was a major controversy during the House-Senate conference on the ADA. Although the original language of the ADA did provide for some coverage for the congressional branch, Congress

---

[68] *Henderson v Bodine Aluminum, Inc.* 70 F.3d 958 (8th Cir. 1995).

[69] *Ouida Sue Parker v. Metropolitan Life Insurance Co.,* 99 F.3d 181, 182 (6th Cir. 1996).

[70] 42 U.S.C. §12212.

expanded upon this in the Congressional Accountability Act, P.L. 104-1. The major area of expansion was the incorporation of remedies that were analogous to those in the ADA applicable to the private sector.[71]

---

[71] For a more detailed discussion of the application of the ADA to Congress see "Congressional Accountability Act of 1995," CRS Rep. No. 95-557A (1995). Congress recently applied the employment and public accommodation provisions of the ADA to the Executive Office of the President. P.L. 104-331 (October 26, 1996).

Chapter 7

THE AMERICANS WITH DISABILITY ACT: POST SUTTON DECISION ON DEFINITION OF DISABILITY

Nancy Lee Jones

INTRODUCTION

The Supreme Court in the landmark decision of *Sutton v. United Air Lines* examined the definition of disability used in the Americans with Disabilities Act (ADA) and found that the determination of whether an individual is disabled should be made with reference to measures that mitigate the individual's impairment. This holding and related ones in other Supreme Court decisions have spawned new issues regarding the definition of disability in recent lower court cases. This chapter will briefly discuss the Supreme Court's opinions and analyze how the lower courts are interpreting the Supreme Court's holdings.

SUPREME COURT DECISIONS

The threshold issue in any ADA case is whether the individual alleging discrimination is an individual with disability. The ADA defines the term disability with respect to an individual as "(A) a physical or mental

impairment that substantially limits one or more of the major life activities of
such individuals; (B) a record of such an impairment; or (C) being regarded
as having such an impairment."[1] The first Supreme Court ADA case to
address this issues was *Bragdon v. Abbott,* a case involving a dentist who
refused to treat an HIV infected individual outside of a hospital.[2] In
Bragdon, the Court found that the plaintiff's asymptomatic HIV infection
was a physical impairment impacting on the major life activity of
reproduction.

Two other cases the Court has decided on the definitional issue involved
whether the effects of medication or assistive devices should be taken into
consideration in determining whether or not an individual has a disability.
The Court in the landmark decision of *Sutton v. United Airlines*[3] and in
Murphy v. United Parcel Service, Inc.,[4] held the "determination of whether
an individual is disabled should be made with reference to measures that
mitigate the individual's impairment...."[5] The *Sutton* Court stated: "a
'disability' exists only where an impairment 'substantially limits' a major
life activity, not where it 'might,' 'could,' or 'would' be substantially
limiting if mitigating measures were not taken." To be substantially limited
in the major life activity of working was seen by the majority as being
precluded from more than one type of job. The Court also emphasized that
the statement of findings in the ADA that some 43,000,000 Americans have
one or more physical or mental disabilities "requires the conclusion that
Congress did not intend to bring under the statute's protection all those
whose uncorrected conditions amount to disabilities." The proper analysis
was described as examining in an individualized manner whether an
individual has a disability. Thus individuals who use prosthetic limbs or a
wheelchair "may be mobile and capable of functioning in society but still be
disabled because of a substantial limitation on their ability to walk or run."

Although the Court's decision in *Sutton* did not turn on the third prong
of the definition of disability (being "regarded as having such an

---

[1] 42 U.S.C. §12102.

[2] 524 U.S. 624 (1998). For a more detailed discussion of this decision see Jones, "The
Americans with Disabilities Act: HIV Infection is Covered Under the Act," CRS Report
98-599 (July 10, 1998).

[3] _U.S._, 119 S.Ct. 2139, 144 L.Ed. 450 (1999).

[4] _U.S._, 119 S.Ct. 2133, 144 L.Ed. 484 (1999).

[5] *Sutton v. United Airlines, supra.* See also *Murphy v. United Parcel Service, supra,* where the
Court held that the determination of whether the petitioner's high blood pressure
substantially limits one or more major life activities must be made considering the
mitigating measures he employs, and *Albertsons Inc. v. Kirkingburg,* _U.S._, 119 S.Ct.
2162, 144 L.Ed.2d 518 (1999), where the Court held unanimously that the ADA requires
proof that the limitation on a major life activity by the impairment is substantial.

impairment") the Court did address the interpretation of this part of the definition. There are two ways, the Court stated, that an individual can fall within the "regarded as" prong: (1) a covered entity mistakenly believes that a person has a physical impairment that substantially limits one or more major life activities, or (2) a covered entity mistakenly believes that an actual impairment substantially limits one or more major life activities. The Court found that, on its own, the allegation that an entity has a vision requirement in place does not establish a claim that the entity regards an individual as substantially impaired in the major life activity of working. The term "substantially limits" was regarded as significant. It requires "at a minimum, that plaintiffs allege they are unable to work in a broad class of jobs." The Court emphasized that it was "assuming without deciding" that working is a major life activity and that the EEOC regulations interpreting "substantially limits" are reasonable[6] and found that even using the EEOC interpretation, the plaintiffs in *Sutton* failed to allege adequately that their vision is regarded as an impairment that substantially limits them in a major life activity. Being precluded from the job of a global airline pilot was not sufficient since they could obtain other, although less lucrative jobs, as regional pilots or pilot instructors.

The "regarded as" prong was directly at issue in *Murphy*. In *Murphy* the Court held that the fact that an individual with high blood pressure was unable to meet the Department of Transportation (DOT) safety standards was not sufficient to create an issue of fact regarding whether an individual is regarded as unable to utilize a class of jobs. Like *Sutton,* the holding in *Murphy* emphasized the numerous other jobs available to the plaintiff.

LOWER COURT DECISIONS SINCE *SUTTON*

Introduction

Although the Supreme Court's decisions on the definition of disability are of recent vintage, they have already spawned numerous lower court cases. The most significant of these are discussed below.

---

[6] It is also important to note that the Court noted that the ADA did not specifically give any agency the authority to interpret the term disability but that because both parties to *Sutton* accepted the regulation as valid "we have no occasion to consider what deference they are due, if any."

Corrective Measures

The mere fact that an individual with a disability uses corrective measures was not seen as barring suit in *Franklin v. Consolidated Edison Co. of New York.*[7] In *Franklin,* an individual with epilepsy who took medication successfully argued that she was and individual with a disability since the medication effected her sleep and work. Similarly, in *Belk v. Southwestern Bell Telephone Co.*[8] the court found that the plaintiff was disabled in the major life activity of walking since he has to wear a leg brace as a result of polio. The employer had argued that since he could walk and engage in many physical activities such as hunting and fishing, he was not disabled. The eighth circuit observed that "unlike the petitioners in *Sutton,* Belk's brace does not allow him to function the same as someone who never had polio. Therefore, he is clearly 'disabled' as defined by the ADA."

However, there are some cases where corrective measures were found to prevent an individual from meeting the definition of an individual with a disability. In *Todd v. Academy Corporation,*[9] an individual with a disability was not found to be disabled since he only had light seizures with his medication. Also, in *Spades v. City of Walnut Ridge*[10] depression was not found to be a disability when it was controlled by medication. And in *Pacella, v. Tufts University School of Dental Medicine,*[11] corrected vision and lack of depth perception were not a substantially limiting disability.

Another issues which has been raised regarding corrective measures is whether an individual with a disability is required to take medication to alleviate his or her condition. In *Spradley v. Custom Campers, Inc.,*[12] the plaintiff worked at the company's manufacturing plant and was terminated for safety reasons after he had seizures at work. On both occasions when the plaintiff had seizures at work, he was not taking medication to control his seizures. The district court, finding in favor of the company, noted that the Supreme Court had held that conditions controlled by corrective measures do not substantially limit a major life activity, implying but not directly stating that the plaintiff had some responsibility to take his medication. However, in *Finical v. Collections Unlimited, Inc.,*[13] a hearing impaired individual alleged that she was fired when she requested a telephone with an amplifying

---

[7] 1999 U.S. Dist. LEXIS 15582 (S.D.N.Y. September 30, 1999).

[8] 194 F.3d 946 (8[Th] Cir. 1999).

[9] 57 F.Supp.2d 448 (S.D. Tex. 1999).

[10] 186 F.3d 897 (8th Cir. 1999). See also *Hall v. Masterlock Co.,* 1999 U.S. Dist. LEXIS 13119 (M.D.Ala. Aug. 12, 1999).

[11] 66 F.Supp.2d 234 (D.Mass. 1999).

[12] 68 F.Supp.2d 1225 (D. Kansas 1999).

[13] 65 F. Supp.2d 1032 (D.Ariz. 1999).

headset. The employer argued that she should be evaluated with a hearing aid but the plaintiff had not used a hearing aid since she had found that it picked up too much background noise. The court rejected the employer's argument finding that *Sutton's* individualized inquiry does not permit an employer to consider the use of corrective devices which are not actually used.

Major Life Activities

As was suggested by the recent Supreme Court decisions, it has proved difficult for plaintiffs to prove that they are limited in the major life activity of working. For example, in *Broussard v. University of California*[14] an employee with carpal tunnel syndrome was not found to be substantially limited in the major life activity of working since she was able to be employed in a wide range of jobs.[15] Similarly, a Utah nurse with multiple sclerosis was not found to be disabled since she was limited in performing one nursing position rather than a broad range of positions.[16] However, in *Fjellestad v. Pizza Hut of America*[17] the eighth circuit examined what it meant to be substantially limited in the major life activity of working and found that a unit manager who suffered a permanent 30% impairment of her upper right extremity was a person with a disability. The court observed that the ADA was concerned with preventing a significant reduction in a person's real work opportunities and phrased the issue as "whether the particular impairment constitutes for the particular person a significant barrier to employment." It was not necessary to show that no employment opportunities existed; statistics showing a 91% reduction in employability and a 95% reduction in labor market access where sufficient.

The ninth circuit addressed the coverage of major life activities in *McAlindin v. County of San Diego.*[18] In *McAlindin,* the court held that sleeping, engaging in sexual relations, and interacting with others are major

---

[14] 192 F.3d 1252 (9th Cir. 1999).

[15] See also, *Paul v. Wisconsin Department of Industry,* 1999 U.S. LEXIS 20362 (Aug. 24, 1999).

[16] *Sorensen v. University of Utah Hospital,* 194 F. 3d 1084 (10th Cir. Oct. 14, 1999). See also, *Avery v. Omaha Public Power District,* 1999 U.S. App. LEXIS 17699 (8th Cir. July 27, 1999), where the eighth circuit found that the plaintiff was not substantially limited in the major life activity of working since he had only shown that the power district regarded him as unable to perform a single position.

[17] 188 F.3d 944 (8th Cir. 1999), rehearing en banc and rehearing denied, 199 U.S. App. LEXIS 25675 (Oct. 13, 1999).

[18] 192 F.3d 1226 (9th Cir. 1999).

life activities under the ADA. This case, however, relied heavily on an earlier Supreme Court interpretation of the ADA in *Bragdon v. Abbott*.[19]

"History of" or "Regarded As"

The second two prongs of the definition of disability under the ADA are having history of a disability or being "regarded as" having a disability. Several commentators predicted that after *Sutton* these two prongs would become increasingly important and it appears that this prediction has been accurate.

Plaintiffs have been successful in several cases under the second and third prongs of the definitions. In *Heyman v. Queens Village Committee for Mental Health*,[20] the second circuit court of appeals held that an individual with asymptomatic lymphoma was "regarded as" having a disability since he was apparently fired from his job after disclosing his condition. The court, in arriving at this holding, observed that a plaintiff cannot make a successful claim under the "regarded as" prong "simply by alleging that the employer believes some physical condition... renders the plaintiff disabled. Rather, the plaintiff must allege that the employer believed, however erroneously, that the plaintiff suffered from an 'impairment' that, if it truly existed, would be covered under the statute and that the employer discriminated against the plaintiff on that basis."

However, not every argument under these parts of the definition has been successful. In *Gorbitz c. Corvilla Inc.*,[21] the seventh circuit court of appeals found that the plaintiff, who had been injured in an auto accident, failed to present evidence that her firing was pretextual. Her numerous doctor's appointments were not sufficient since they did not by themselves signal the existence of a disability.

---

[19] 524 U.S. 624 (1998). But see *Gutwaks v. American Airlines*, 1999 U.S. Dist. LEXIS 16833 (N.D.Tex. Sept. 2, 1999), where the court found that the plaintiff's HIV status did not qualify him as an individual with a disability. The plaintiff testified that he had never had a desire to father children, unlike the plaintiff in *Bragdon*, and the court concluded the "while HIV positivity clearly is a disability under the Ada when it limits a major life activity, it is apparent here that reproduction is not a major life activity for Gutwaks.

[20] 1999 U.S. App. LEXIS 30720 (2d Cir. Nov. 30, 1999).

[21] 196 F. 3d 879 (7th Cir. 1999).

Chapter 8

THE AMERICANS WITH DISABILITIES ACT: SUPREME COURT TO HEAR CASE INVOLVING HIV INFECTION

Nancy Lee Jones

INTRODUCTION

The Supreme Court has granted certiorari in *Bragdon v. Abbott,* 107 F.3d 934 (1st Cir. 1997), *cert. granted* 66 U.S.L.W. 3384 (Nov. 26, 1997). Oral argument will be heard in late March and the Court is expected to decide the case by the end of the term. This will be the first time the Supreme Court interprets the Americans with Disabilities Act (ADA) and it will do so in the context of a case involving the refusal by a dentist to perform certain invasive procedures on an HIV infected individual in his office. The first circuit court of appeals found that the dentist's actions violated the ADA. Three specific questions are presented to the Supreme Court: (1) is reproduction a major life activity under the ADA; (2) are asymptomatic individuals infected with HIV individuals with a disability under the ADA; and (3) should courts defer to the professional judgment of a health care provider when deciding whether a private health care provider must perform invasive procedures on an infectious patient in his or her office? This report discusses the lower court decision in *Bragdon,* the applicable ADA requirements, and the potential implications of the decision for ADA decisions in related areas.

In 1994 Dr. Bragdon performed a dental examination on Ms. Abbott and discovered a cavity. M.S. Abbott had indicated on her registration form that she was HIV positive. At the time, she was asymptomatic. Dr. Bragdon told her that he would not fill her cavity in his office but would treat her only in a hospital setting. This would have resulted in higher costs for Ms. Abbott since, although Dr. Bragdon would have charged his regular fee, she would have had to have paid the hospital costs.[1] Ms. Abbott did not find this acceptable and filed a complaint under the ADA, 42 U.S.C. §§1201 et seq., a broad civil rights statute that prohibits discrimination against individuals with disabilities. She prevailed at the district court and court of appeals levels. The Supreme Court then granted certiorari and accepted three specific questions for review: whether reproduction is a major life activity, whether asymptomatic individuals infected with HIV are individuals with a disability under when deciding whether a private health care provider must perform invasive procedures on an infectious patient in his or her office.[2]

THE AMERICANS WITH DISABILITIES ACT

The Americans with Disabilities Act, 42 U.S.C. §§ 12101 et seq; provide broad nondiscrimination protection for individuals with disabilities in employment, public services, public accommodation and services operated by private entities, transportation and telecommunications.[3] The ADA state that "the term 'disability' means, with respect to an individual – (A) a physical or mental impairment that substantially limits one or more of the major life activities of such individuals; (B) a record of such an impairment; or (C) being regarded as having such an impairment."[4] Although discrimination against such individuals is prohibited in places of public accommodations such as doctor's offices,[5] there are some limitations

---

[1] In addition, the respondent's brief indicates that Dr. Bragdon had not applied for hospital privileges at this time and only applied after Ms. Abbott filed a complaint with the Maine Human Rights Commission. The hospital Dr. Bragdon applied to for privileges was two hours from his office.

[2] 66 U.S.L.W. 3384 (Nov. 26, 1997); 66 U.S.L.W 3134 (Aug. 12, 1997).

[3] For a more detailed discussion of the ADA see Jones, "The Americans with Disabilities Act (ADA): An Overview of Major Provisions and Issues," CRS Rept. 97-242A (Feb. 12, 1997).

[4] 42 U.S.C. §12102(2).

[5] 42 U.S.C. § 12181.

on the reach of this nondiscrimination requirement. The most significant of these limitations with regard to the issues presented by *Bragdon* is the exception for situations that pose a direct threat to the health or safety of others. The term "direct threat" is defined in the statute as "a significant risk to the health or safety of others that cannot be eliminated by a modification of policies, practices, or procedures or by the provision of auxiliary aids or services."[6] It was created in an attempt to differentiate legitimate public health concerns from prejudicial stereotypes.

FIRST CIRCUIT OF APPEALS DECISION

The first circuit court of appeals began its opinion with an analysis of the definition of disability. With regard to the requirement of an impairment, the first circuit found that "HIV-positive status... whether symptomatic or asymptomatic, comprises a physical impairment under the ADA."[7] The first circuit spent more time analyzing whether HIV-positive status adversely affects a major life activity. Ms. Abbott argued that reproduction was the major life activity affected while Dr. Bragdon argued that reproduction cannot be considered a major life activity because it is essentially a life style choice. The court examined other ADA decisions, several of which found that reproduction was not a major life activity, but held that "(t)hough the question is very close, we think it must be resolved favorably to Ms. Abbott. Reproduction... constitutes a major life activity because of its singular importance to those who engage in it, both in terms of its significance in their lives and in terms of its relation to their day-to-day existence."[8] In addition, the court rejected the claim that Ms. Abbott was not disabled under the ADA unless reproduction was a major life activity for her.

The next legal issue addressed by the court of appeals was whether the HIV infection substantially limits the major life activity of reproduction. All the parties conceded that with AZT therapy an infected woman had an 8% risk or transmitting the virus to her child. Dr. Bragdon argued that this risk did not substantially limit the major life activity of reproduction. The first circuit did not find this argument convincing. The 8% risk was considered significant and, in addition, the court noted that even if Ms. Abbott gave birth to a healthy child, she was not likely to live long enough to raise the child to adulthood.

---

[6] *Id.*
[7] *Abbott v. Bragdon*, 107 F.3d 934, 939 (1st Cir. 1997).
[8] *Id.* at 941.

The legislative history of the ADA was also seen as supportive of the court's holding. The court noted that the House report stated: "Persons infected with the Human Immunodeficiency Virus are considered to have an impairment that substantially limits a major life activity, and thus are considered disabled under the first test of the definition."[9] In addition, the court observed that the Department of Justice had interpreted the Rehabilitation Act, the statute upon which the ADA was based, as protecting individuals with HIV infection.[10]

The next issue presented to the court was whether Dr. Bragdon was protected by the exception to the ADA for situations that pose "a direct threat to the health or safety of others."[11] In finding that the direct threat standard was not applicable in this case, the court of appeals found that deference should be given to public health officials but that the conclusions of public health officials "may be rebutted by persuasive evidence adduced from other recognized experts in a given field."[12] The direct threat defense was not to be used to mask prejudice. "Under the ADA, a service provider like Dr. Bragdon is not entitled to demand absolute safety; he can rely upon the direct threat defense only in response to significant risks."[13]

In its conclusion, the first circuit court of appeals emphasized the difficult decisions posed by the case. The case was seen as "necessarily fact sensitive"[14] and the court noted that if the facts changed, for example by dramatic improvements in medical science that substantially reduced the likelihood of transmitting HIV to a fetus, the court's holding may change as well. The first circuit cautioned future courts not to read the decision broadly but rather as an example of case-by-case inquiry into a dentist's responsibility to treat HIV infected patients.

---

[9] *Id.* at 943, quoting H.Rep. No. 101-485(III) at 28 n. 18 (1990), *reprinted in* 1990 USCCAN 445, 451 n. 18.

[10] *Id.* at 943.

[11] 42 U.S.C. §12182(b)(3).

[12] *Abbott v. Bragdon,* 107 F.3d 934, 945 (1st Cir. 1997).

[13] *Id.* at 948.

[14] *Id.* at 949.

OTHER LOWER COURT DECISIONS ON
ISSUES BEFORE THE SUPREME COURT

One of the reasons the Supreme Court's decision in *Bragdon* may be significant is that many of the issues the Supreme Court has before it relate to issues presented in other cases. The Court's decision could affect the decisions of cases involving whether reproduction is a major life activity, whether asymptomatic individuals are covered by the ADA, and how direct threat limitation is to be interpreted.

The lower courts are split on the issue of whether reproduction is a major life activity under the ADA. Several courts, including the eighth circuit in *Krauel v. Iowa Methodist Medical Center,* 95 F.3d 694 (8th Cir. 1996), have found that the ability to reproduce is not a major life activity. In *Krauel* the court reasoned that since it was undisputed that the plaintiff's infertility did not prevent her from performing her full job duties, it was "a considerable stretch of federal law" to find that infertility was a disability.[15] On the other hand, the first circuit in *Brandon* came to the opposite conclusion as did other district courts.[16] Obviously, a ruling by the Supreme Court concerning reproduction as a disability could be dispositive of this issues.

With regard to whether asymptomatic individuals are covered by the ADA, the closest factual situation is that in *Runnebaum v. Nations Bank of Maryland,* 123 f.3d 156 (4th Cir. 1997). In *Runnebaum,* an employee sued his former employer alleging that he had been fired due to his asymptomatic HIV infection. The fourth circuit held that the employee did not meet the definition of an individual with a disability under the ADA since he was asymptomatic. "Extending the coverage of the ADA to asymptomatic conditions like Runnebaum's where no diminishing effects are exhibited, would run counter to Congress's intention as expressed in the plain statutory language."[17] Interestingly, the fourth circuit quoted from the ADA Committee Reports which listed infection with HIV as included within the term mental or physical impairments. However, the court found that the statutory language was clear and that there was no need to refer to the legislative history and that even of the legislative history was examined it

---

[15] See also *Zatarain v. WDSU-Television,* 881 F.Supp. 240 (E.D.La. 1995).

[16] See e.g., *Soodman v. Wildman, Harrold, Allen & Dixon,* 1997 U.S. Dist. LEXIS 1495 (N.D.III.Feb. 10, 1997).

[17] *Runnebaum v. NationsBank of Maryland,* 123 F.3d 156, 168 (4th Cir. 1997).

was not dispositive since it did not distinguish between symptomatic and asymptomatic conditions.

If the Supreme Court were to adopt the reasoning in *Runnebaum*, it could have implications far beyond the provision of dental services to HIV infected individuals. Any condition which is asymptomatic could be affected. For example, the second circuit recently ruled that a woman with ulcerative colitis was not individual with a disability since she was asymptomatic most of the time and the court found that this weight against finding that she had a substantial limitation on a major life activity.[18] If the Court adopted the *Runnebaum* reasoning regarding coverage of asymptomatic individuals, cases like this one would be upheld.

The issue of how the direct threat language in the ADA is interpreted will also be significant. In *School Broad of Nasau County v. Airline*, 480 U.S. 273 (1987), the Supreme Court addressed the issue of dangerousness in the context of section 504 of the Rehabilitation Act of 1973, 29 U.S.C. §794. Section 504 prohibits discrimination against individuals with disabilities in any program or activity that received federal financial assistance and was used as the model for the ADA. In *Arline* the Supreme Court held that section 504 covered contagious diseases that substantially limit one or more of an individual's major life activities, in that case, breathing. However, in order to determine whether an individual with a contagious disease is otherwise qualified for a job or program, the Supreme Court found that courts should conduct a factual inquiry based on "reasonable medical judgments given the state of medical knowledge, about (a) the nature of the risk (how the disease is transmitted), (b) the duration of the risk (how long is the carrier infectious), (c) the severity of the risk (what is the potential harm to third parties) and (d) the probabilities the disease will be transmitted and will cause varying degrees of harm.[19] The Supreme Court's decision in *Bragdon* may provide guidance on how these factors are to be interpreted under the ADA. Of perhaps most importance, the Court will have the opportunity to determine the deference that should be accorded to the views of public health officials.

---

[18] *Ryan v. Grae & Rybicki P.C.*, No. 96-9681 (2d Cir. Feb. 4, 1998). In addition, individuals with genetic predispositions for serious diseases but who were otherwise healthy could arguably be excluded under the *Runnebaum* reasoning.

[19] *School Board of Nassau County v. Airline*, 480 U.S. 273, 288 (1987).

Chapter 9

AMERICANS WITH DISABILITIES ACT: REGULATIONS AND INFORMATION SOURCES

Andre O. Mander[1]

INTRODUCTION

The Americans with Disabilities Act (ADA), Pub. Law No. 101-336, prohibits discrimination against individuals with disabilities in employment, public services, public accommodations and services operated by private entities, transportation and telecommunications. Numerous regulations have been promulgated under the ADA. This chapter contains citations to these regulations, telephone numbers and internet web sites (if available) where copies of and/or information about the regulations may be obtained, and telephone numbers and internet web sites (if available) of organizations which may be of assistance to constituents.[2] TDD numbers are included when available.

---

[1] Nancy Jones, Legislative Attorney, supervised the production of this chapter.

[2] The inclusion of an organization on this list does not constitute an endorsement by the Congressional Research Service or the Library of Congress of these organizations or of any interpretations of the Americans with Disabilities Act offered by them. It should also be emphasized that this list is representative, not exhaustive, and that the non-inclusion of an organization on the list is not a comment on the organization or its services.

REGULATIONS UNDER THE AMERICANS WITH DISABILITIES ACT (ADA) AS OF JUNE 6, 1997.

Executive Branch

Architectural and Transportation Barriers Compliance Board
Regulation: Accessibility guidelines for buildings and facilities.
Cite: 36 C.F.R. § 1191 (1997)
Regulation: Accessibility guidelines for transportation facilities.
Cite: 36 C.F.R. § 1192 (1997)
               (800)-872-2253-Voice
               (202)-272-5449-TDD
               www.access-board.gov.

Department of Justice
Regulation: Delegated authority of Attorney General under ADA to Assistant Attorney General, Civil Rights Division.
Cite: 28 C.F.R. § 0.50 (1997)
Regulation: Nondiscrimination by public accommodations and in commercial facilities.
Cite: 28 C.F.R. § 36 (1997)
Regulation: Nondiscrimination in state and local services.
Cite: 28 C.F.R. § 35(1997)
               (800)-514-0301-Voice
               (800)-514-0383-TDD
               www.usdoj.gov/crt/ada/adahom1

Department of Transportation
Regulation: Transportation for individuals with disabilities.
Cite: 49 C.F.R. §§ 37-38 (1997)
               (202)-366-9306-Voice
               (202)-755-7687-TDD

Equal Employment Opportunity Commission
Regulation: Procedural regulations for enforcement of Title I (employment) of AdA.
Cite: 29 C.F.R. § 1601 (1997)
Regulation: Available of records

Cite: 29 C.F.R. § 1610 (1997)
Regulation: Equal employment opportunity for individuals with disabilities.
Cite: 29 C.F.R. § 1630 (1997)
Regulation: Recordkeeping and reporting under title VII and ADA.
Cite: 29 C.F.R. §§ 1602, 1627
             (202)-663-4900-Voice
             (202)-663-4141-TDD
             For ordering documents (print or other formats):
             (800)-669-3362-Voice
             (800)-800-3302-TDD

Federal Communications Commission
Regulation: Telecommunications services for hearing and speech disabled.
Cite: 47 C.F.R. §§ 0.91, 64.601-64.608 (1997)
             (202)-418-2335-Voice
             (202)-418-0484-TDD

President's Committee on Employment of People with Disability
             General employment information and publications.
             (202)-376-6200-Voice
             (202)-376-6205-TDD
             www.pcepd.gov.

Legislative Branch

Office of Compliance
Regulation: Extension of rights and protections of the ADA.
Cite: 143 Cong. Rec. S30-61 (daily ed. January 7, 1997)
             (Notice of Adoption and Submission for Approval)
             (202)-724-9250-Voice
             (202)-426-1912-TDD

OTHER SOURCES OF INFORMATION AND ASSISTANCE

The Arc

The national association is an advocacy, support and information group for children and adults with mental retardation.
(800)-433-5255-Voice
(817)-277-0553-TDD
www.theArc.org

American Civil Liberties Union

General ADA information
212-944-9800-Voice
www.aclu.rg.

American Foundation for the Blind

Promotes "enabling the blind or visually impaired persons to achieve equality of access and opportunity that will ensure freedom in their lives."
(202)-223-0101-Voice/TDD
(800)-232-5463-Voice

Association on Higher Education and Diversity (AHEAD)

Information regarding examinations compliance, ADA compliance of boards of licensure and certification, student service programs, and postsecondary education.
(614)-488-4972-Voice/TDD

United Cerebral Palsy Associations

A national network of state and local affiliates that assists individuals with cerebral palsy and other developmental disabilities and their families.

(800)-872-5827-Voice/TDD
www.ucpa.org.

Disability Rights Education and Defense Fund (DREDF)

General ADA provisions training, technical assistance, public policy advocacy and litigation.
(202)-986-0375-Voice
(510)-644-2626-TDD

Job Accommodation Network

Provides information on job accommodations and the employability of people with functional limitations.
(800)-526-7234-Voice/TDD
www.jan.wvu.edu.

Bazelon Center for Mental Health Law

Information regarding disability laws with emphasis on persons who are mentally ill.
(202)-467-5730-Voice
(202)-467-4232-TDD
www.bazelon.org

National Association of the Deaf

Promotes the rights of those who are deaf or hard of hearing.
(301)-587-1788-Voice
(301)-587-1789-TDD
www.nad.org.

National Conference of States on Building Codes and Standards

Promotes certification of states codes for equivalency with ADA standards and promotes the development of alternative dispute resolution procedures within the existing state regulatory framework.
(703)-437-0100-Voice
(703)-481-2019-TDD

National Association of Protection and Advocacy Systems

Organization of agencies working for the rights of the mentally ill or developmentally disabled and clients of the vocational rehabilitation system.
(202)-408-9514-Voice
(202)-408-9521-TDD

National Council on Disability

Advises law makers and produces publications tracking federal laws and programs affecting people with disabilities.
(202)-272-2004-Voice
(202)-202-2074-TDD

National Easter Seal Society

Federation of state and local groups with programs that help people with disabilities achieve independence.
(202)-347-3066-Voice
(202)-347-7385-TDD

National Information Center for Children and Youth with Disabilities (NICHCY)

Information and referral service for people with disabilities, their families and professionals.
(800)-695-0285-Voice
www.nichcy.org.

National Rehabilitation Information Center

Information or rehabilitation and training.
(800)-346-2742-Voice

Regional Disability and Business Technical Assistance Center

Provides technical assistance in implementation of the ADA for business and others through regional centers.
(800)-949-4232-Voice/TDD

Chapter 10

THE AMERICANS WITH DISABILITY NOTIFICATION ACT, H.R. 3590

Nancy Lee Jones

INTRODUCTION

The Americans with Disability Act (ADA), 42 U.S.C. §12101 *et seq.,* provides broad nondiscrimination protection in employment, public services, public accommodation and services operated by private entities, transportation, and telecommunications. H.R. 3590, 106th Congress, the ADA Notification Act, would amend title III of the ADA, which contains the provisions relating to public accommodations, to require that a plaintiff provide 90 days notice to the defendant prior to filing a complaint. Hearings were held on May 18, 2000.

THE AMERICANS WITH DISABILITIES ACT

The Americans with Disabilities Act has often been described as the most sweeping nondiscrimination legislation since the Civil Rights Act of 1964. As stated in the Act, its purpose is "to provide clear and comprehensive national mandate for the elimination of discrimination against individuals with disabilities."[1]

Title III provides that no individuals shall be discriminated against on the basis of disability in the full and equal enjoyment of the goods, services, facilities, privileges, advantages, or accommodations of any place of public accommodation by any person who owns, leases (or leases to), or operates a place of public accommodation.[2] Entities covered by the term "public accommodation" are listed and include, among others, hotels, restaurants, theaters, auditoriums, laundromats, museums, parks, zoos, private schools, day care centers, professional offices of health care providers, and gymnasiums.[3] Although the sweep of title III is broad, there are some limitations on its nondiscrimination requirements. A failure to remove architectural barriers is not a violation unless such a removal is "readily achievable."[4] "Readily achievable" is defined as "easily accomplishable and able to be carried out without much difficulty or expense."[5] Reasonable modifications in practices, polices or procedures are required unless they would fundamentally alter the nature of the goods, services, facilities, or privileges or they would result in an undue burden.[6] An undue burden is defined as an action involving "significant difficulty or expense."[7]

The remedies and procedures of section 204(a) of the Civil Rights Act of 1964 are incorporated in title III of the ADA.[8] This allows for both private suit and suit by the Attorney General when there is reasonable cause to believe that there is a pattern or practice of discrimination against individuals with disabilities. Monetary damages are not recoverable in private suits but may be available in suits brought by the Attorney General.[9] The impact of these provisions on small businesses was of concern to Congress when the ADA was enacted. Generally, title III provisions were not to become effective for eighteen months and there were specific further extensions for small businesses concerning the requirements for new construction and alteration. Actions under section 303 of the ADA were not allowed during the first six months after the effective date for businesses that employed 25

---

[1] 42 U.S.C. §12102(b)(1).
[2] 42 U.S.C. §12182.
[3] 42 U.S.C. §12181.
[4] 42 U.S.C. §12182(b)(2)(A)(iv).
[5] 42 U.S.C. §12181.
[6] 42 U.S.C. §12182(b)(2)(A).
[7] 28 C.F.R. §36.104.
[8] 42 U.S.C. §12188. Section 204a-3(a) of the Civil Rights Act of 1964 is codified at 42 U.S.C. §2000a-3(a).
[9] 42 U.S.C. §12188(b)(4).

or fewer and have gross receipts of $1,000,000 or less. Similarly, section 303 actions were not allowed during the first year after the effective date against businesses that employed 10 or fewer employees and had gross receipts of $500,000 or less.[10]

Section 204(c) of the Civil Rights Act requires that when there is a state or local law prohibiting an action also prohibited by title II, no civil action may be brought "before the expiration of thirty days after written notice of such alleged act or practice has been given to the appropriate State or local authority...." Although the ADA does not specifically incorporate this requirement, several courts have found that it was a prerequisite to suit.[11]

H.R. 3590

The ADA Notification Act, H.R. 3590, would add provisions to the remedies and procedures of title III of the ADA to require a plaintiff to provide notice of an alleged violation to the defendant. This notice may be provided by registered mail or in person and shall contain the specific facts regarding the alleged violation including the identification of the location at which the violation occurred, and the date on which the violation occurred. This notice also shall inform the defendant that civil action may not be commenced until the expiration of a ninety day period. A court does not have jurisdiction unless this notice is provided, at least ninety days have passed, and the complaint states that the defendant has not corrected the alleged violation. If these requirements are not met when a civil action is failed, the court shall impose an appropriate sanction on the attorneys involved. If the criteria are subsequently met and the action proceeds, the court may not award attorneys' fees.

Department of Justice Views on H.R. 3590

The Department of Justice did not testify at the hearings but has gone on record as opposing H.R. 3590. In a letter sent to Rep. Canady, Assistant Attorney General Robert Raben argued that the bill "would work to undermine voluntary compliance with the Americans with Disabilities Act

---

[10] 42 U.S.C. §12181 note.

[11] See e.g. *Synder v. San Diego Flowers*, 21 F. Supp.2d 1207 (S.D.Cal. 1998). However, other courts have found no such requirement. See e.g., *Mirando v. Villa Roma Resorts, Inc.*, 1999 U.S. Dist. LEXIS 17887 (S.D.N.Y. Nov. 18, 1999).

and … would unduly burden legitimate ADA enforcement activity."[12] He noted that if attorneys are engaging in frivolous or harassing litigation the appropriate mechanism for addressing such problems is with the ethics and disciplinary bodies of state bar associations or the court where the litigation is pending. In addition, he detailed the efforts the Department of Justice has made to provide technical assistance.[13]

Hearing Testimony in Favor of H.R. 3590

The ADA Notification Act attempts to prevent what its supporters have described as "drive by lawsuits." In his testimony, Representative Foley, who along with Rep. Shaw, introduced the bill, noted that the ADA was an important piece of civil rights legislation but stated that "to put it simply, the ADA is being used by some attorneys to shake down thousands of businesses from Florida to California."[14] Rep. Foley observed that title III of the ADA does not allow for the collection of damages by plaintiffs but does allow for attorneys' fees and stated that "some attorneys apparently have figured out that the ADA can be a real cash cow for minimum work on their part."[15] He cited the actions of a group in Florida that "filed a blizzard of lawsuits against dozens of businesses" as exemplifying the reason for H.R. 3590.

One of the most prominent supporters of H.R. 3590, Clint Eastwood, testified in support of the legislation at hearings, noting that he had been sued because a hotel he owned was not in compliance with the ADA. The suit against his Mission Ranch Hotel and Restaurant alleged that at least one bathroom and the hotel parking lot did not comply with the ADA and asked for $577,000 in attorneys' fees. Like the bill's sponsors, Mr. Eastwood argued that he and other small businesses were being "preyed upon by money seeking attorneys."[16]

Christopher Bell, the managing partner of a national management labor and employment law firm, also argued in support of H.R. 3590. He described

---

[12] Letter to Honorable Charles Canady, Chairman, Subcommittee on the Constitution, House Committee on the Judiciary from Robert Raben, Assistant Attorney General, reprinted at [http://www.jfanow.org/cgi/getli.pl?1063]

[13] Id.

[14] Testimony of the Honorable Mark Foley, H.R. 3590, the ADA Notification Act Before the House Committee on the Judiciary, Subcommittee on the Constitution, May 18, 2000. Published at [http://www.house.gov/judiciary/fole0518.htm.]

[15] Id.

[16] "Clint Eastwood Battles Disabled Advocates," *USA Today* (May 18, 2000) [http://www.usatoday.com/news/wasdc/ncsthu01.htm]

ADA "drive by suits" as "all too common" with four major "ADA enforcement groups" having filed 112 lawsuits since January 1, 2000. Mr. Bell concluded that H.R. 3590 "does not make any substantive legal changes to the ADA. It does not reduce in any way or to any degree the substantive rights or persons with disabilities."

Several witnesses testified concerning their specific knowledge regarding certain lawsuits. Tammy Fields, testifying on behalf of the Palm Beach County Board of County Commissioners, stated that the County Commissioners adopted a resolution urging passage of the H.R. 3590. This occurred after thirty-eight law suits were filed by one law firm in a two week period against small businesses in a depressed area.[17] Donna and David Batelaan testified that they were the co-owners of a mobility equipment business in Florida and had mobility impairments themselves. They lauded the purposes and effects of the ADA without which "we may not have been able to come here today to testify" but argued for notice for small businesses so they would not be subjected to large attorneys' fees.[18] Terri Lynn Davis, a manager or a commercial office and retail center and volunteer for a group raising money for United Cerebral Palsy, testified about her experience in being sued for having six instead of seven parking places available for individuals with disabilities.[19]

Hearing Testimony in Opposition to H.R. 3590

Although the actions of some attorneys are almost universally deplored, there is considerable disagreement concerning whether the approach taken by H.R. 3590 is appropriate. One of the hearing witnesses, "will make enforcement of the ADA cumbersome, much more expensive, and from a practical standpoint, frequently impossible. Worse, it will eliminate much of the existing incentive businesses have to attempt to comply with the law

---

[17] Testimony of Tammy K. Fields, H.R. 3590, the ADA Notification Act Before the House Committee on the Judiciary, Subcommittee on the Constitution, May 18, 2000. Published at [http://www.house.gov/judiciary/tfie0518.htm.] See also, Testimony of Joseph R. Fields, Jr., H.R. 3590, the ADA Notification Act Before the House Committee on the Judiciary, Subcommittee on the Constitution, May 18, 2000. Published at [http://www.house.gov/judiciary/fie10518.htm]

[18] Testimony of Donna M. Batelaan and David Batelaan, H.R. 3590, the ADA Notification Act Before the House Committee on the Judiciary, Subcommittee on the Constitution, May 18, 2000. Published at [http://www.house.gov/judiciary/bate01518.htm]

[19] Testimony of Terri Lynn Davis, H.R. 3590, the ADA Notification Act Before the House Committee on the Judiciary, Subcommittee on the Constitution, May 18, 2000. Published at [http://www.house.gov/judiciary/davi0518.htm]

voluntarily."[20] He noted that there was no damage provision in the law and observed that since there was no risk of damages, "the effect of prohibiting lawsuits unless they get 90 days notice is to allow – indeed, encourage – them to do nothing until they get a letter."[21] He also observed that attorneys' fees are only available if the plaintiff wins and are limited to what the judge finds is "reasonable" and that the Department of Justice has significant technical assistance available for small businesses. In addition, Mr. Levy questioned the attorneys' fees Mr. Eastwood indicated were involved in his case stating: "The fees could only have grown to the size they did because of this refusal to comply with the law voluntarily and the scorched earth manner in which his lawyer conducted the defense."[22]

Another witness, Fred Shotz, the ADA consultant for the City of Lake Worth, Florida, also argued against the legislation, stating "[t]he ADA is not broken and it does not need to be fixed."[23] Mr. Shotz made several specific arguments. First, he stated that the bill would have much broader impact than described and would affect all businesses, not simply small business. He observed that there are various categories of lawsuits under title III of the ADA, including suits involving new construction, additions to existing facilities, alterations to existing facilities, accessible route improvements, and architectural barrier removal in entities of various sizes. Of these types of suits, Mr. Shotz stated that only architectural barrier removal in facilities owned by small partnerships and individuals would possibly be worthy of the protections of the legislation. He also argued the bill would require every individual with a disability to know the details regarding ADA access requirements and would limit an individual's ability to obtain legal representation.[24] Mr. Shotz noted that he was aware of several law firms that were "taking advantage of disability laws." He felt that this problem could be addressed by the ethical requirements of the Bar and the authority of district court judges.

---

[20] Testimony of Andrew D. Levy, H.R. 3590, the ADA Notification Act Before the House Committee on the judiciary, Subcommittee on the Constitution, May 18, 2000. Published at [http://www.house.gov/judiciary/levy0518.htm]

[21] *Id.*

[22] *Id.*

[23] Testimony of Fred Shotz, H.R. 3590, the ADA Notification Act Before the House Committee on the Judiciary, Subcommittee on the Constitution, May 18, 2000. Published at [http://www.house.gov/judiciary/shot0518.htm]

[24] *Id.* Mr. Shotz gave an example of how the legislation would work if an individual with quadriplegia encounters an inaccessible restaurant. He stated that she would have to go to the library to find the details for the width of a door and then go back to the restaurant to measure the door and either pay a lawyer to write a letter or write one herself and go to the Post Office to mail the letter certified mail. Then she must go back to the restaurant after 90 days to determine if the condition has been corrected.

Dr. Stewen Rattner, a dentist who has been deaf from birth, also testified against the legislation arguing that adding the notice provision would create significant barriers to obtaining accommodations such as sign language interpreters for continuing education classes.[25] Similarly, Christine Griffin, the executive director of the Disability Law Center, gave examples of several situations where she felt a notification requirement would be problematic.[26]

---

[25] Testimony of Dr. Steven Rattner, H.R.. 3590, the ADA Notification Act Before the House Committee on the Judiciary, Subcommittee on the Constitution, May 18, 2000. Published at [http:/www.house.gov/judiciary/ratt0518.htm]

[26] Testimony of Christine Griffin, H.R. 3590, the ADA Notification Act Before the House Committee on the Judiciary, Subcommittee on the Constitution, May 18, 2000. Published at [http://www.house.gov/judiciary/grif0518.htm] See also Testimony of Kyle Glozier, H.R. 3590, the ADA Notification Act Before the House Committee on the Judiciary, Subcommittee on the Constitution, May 18, 2000. Published at [http://www.house.gov/judiciary/gloz0518.htm]

Chapter 11

THE AMERICANS WITH DISABILITIES ACT (ADA): STATUTORY LANGUAGE AND RECENT ISSUES

Nancy Lee Jones

INTRODUCTION

The Americans with Disabilities Act, ADA, provides broad nondiscrimination protection in employment, public services, public accommodations and services operated by public entities, transportation, and telecommunications for individuals with disabilities. The Supreme Court had decided fifteen ADA cases, including four cases in the 2001-2002 Supreme Court term. This chapter will summarize the major provisions of the ADA and will discuss selected recent issues, including the Supreme Court cases. It will be updated as development warrant.

BACKGROUND

The Americans with Disabilities Act, ADA, 42 U.S.C. §§1201 *et seq.,* has often been described as the most sweeping nondiscrimination legislation since the Civil Rights Act of 1964. It provides broad nondiscrimination protection in employment, public services, public accommodation and services operated by private entities, transportation, and telecommunications for individuals with disabilities. As stated in the Act, its purpose is "to provide a clear and comprehensive national mandate for the elimination of discrimination against individuals with disabilities."[1] Enacted on July 26, 1990, the majority of the ADA's provisions took effect in 1992 but the body of law interpreting the ADA is still being created. The Supreme Court has decided fifteen ADA cases, twelve since 1998.[2] In the 2001-2002 term, the Court decided four ADA cases, *U.S. Airways Inc. v. Barnett, Toyota Motor Manufacturing, Kentucky Inc. v. William, Chevron U.S.A., Inc. v. Echazabal and Barnes v. Gorman.* All of these cases have narrowed scope of the ADA. Three cases involved employment issues and all three cases have limited the rights of employees.

Before examining the provisions of the ADA and these cases, it is important to briefly note the ADA's historical antecedents. A federal statutory provision which existed prior to the ADA, section 504 of the Rehabilitation Act of 1973, prohibits discrimination against an otherwise qualified individual with a disability, solely on the basis of the disability, in any program or activity that receives federal financial assistance, the executive agencies or the U.S. Postal Service.[3] Many of the concepts used in the ADA originated in section 504 and its interpretations; however, there is one major difference. While section 504's prohibition against discrimination is tied to the receipt of federal financial assistance, the ADA also covers entities not receiving such funds. In addition, the federal executive agencies and the U.S. Postal Service are covered under section 504, not the ADA. The ADA contains a specific provision stating that except as otherwise provided in the Act, nothing in the Act shall be construed to apply a lesser standard

---

[1] 42 U.S.C. §12102(b)(1).

[2] *Bragdon v. Abbott,* 524 U.S. 624 (1998): *Pennsylvania Department of Prisons v. Yeskey,* 524 U.S. 206 (1998); *Wright v Universal Maritime Service Corp.,* 525 U.S. 70 (1998); *Cleveland v. Policy Management Systems,* 526 U.S. 795 (1998); *Olmstead v. L.C.,* 527 U.S. 581 (1999); *Murphy v. United Parcel Service, Inc.,* 527 U.S. 516 (1999); *Sutton v. United Air Lines, Inc.,* 527 U.S. 471 (1999); *Kirkingburg v. Albertson's Inc.,* 527 U.S. 555 (1999); *Garrett v. University of Alabama,* 531 U.S. 356 (2001); *PGA Tour v. Martin,*532 U.S. 661 (2001); *Buckhannon Board and Care Home., Inc. v. West Virginia Department of Human Resources,* 532 U.S. 598 (2001); *U.S. Airways Inc. v. Barnett,* 152 L.Ed. 2d 589; 122 S.Ct. 1516; 70 U.S.L.W. 4285 (April 2002); *Toyota Motor Manufacturing v. Williams,* 534 U.S. 184 (2002); *Chevron USA Inc. v. Echazabal,* 122 S.Ct. 2045; 153 L.Ed.2d 82 (2002); and *Barnes v. Gorman,* 122 S.Ct. 2057; 153 L.Ed.2d 230 (2002). The three cases decided in 1998 were *Bragdon v. Abbott,* 524 U.S. 624 (1998); *Pennsylvania Department of Prisons v. Yeskey,* 524 U.S. 624 (1998); *Pennsylvania Department of Prisons v. Yeskey,* 524 U.S.206 (1998); and *Wright v. Universal Maritime Service Corporation,* 525 U.S. 70 (1998). For a discussion limited to Supreme Court decisions on the ADA see Jones, "The Americans with Disabilities Act (ADA): Supreme Court Decisions," RS20246.

[3] 29 U.S.C. §794.

than the standards applied under title V of the Rehabilitation Act (which includes section 504) or the regulations issued by federal agencies pursuant to such title.[4]

The ADA is a civil rights statute; it does not provide grant funds to help entities comply with its requirements. It does include a section on technical assistance which authorizes grants and awards for the purpose of technical assistance such as the dissemination of information about rights under the ADA and techniques for effective compliance.[5] However, there are tax code provisions which may assist certain businesses or individuals.[6]

DEFINITION OF DISABILITY

Statutory Language

The definitions in the ADA, particularly the definition of "disability," are the starting point for an analysis of rights provided by the law. The term "disability," with respect to an individual, is defined as "(A) a physical or mental impairment that substantially limits one or more of the major life activities of such individual; (B) a record of such an impairment; or (C) being regarded as having such an impairment."[7] This definition, which has been the subject of numerous cases brought under the ADA including major Supreme Court decisions, is drawn from the definitional section applicable to section 504.[8]

The definition of "disability" was further elaborated in title V of the ADA. Section 510 provides that the term "individual with a disability" in the ADA does not include an individual who is currently engaging in the illegal use of drugs when the covered entity acts on the basis of such use.[9] An individual who has been rehabilitated would be covered. However, the conference report language clarifies that the provision does not permit individuals to invoke coverage simply by showing they are participating in a drug rehabilitation program; they must refrain from using drugs.[10] The

---

[4] 42 U.S.C. § 12201(a).
[5] 42 U.S.C. § 12206.
[6] See Louis Alan Talley, "Business Tax Provisions that Benefit Persons with Disabilities," CRS Report RS21006; Louis Alan Talley, "Additional Standard Tax Deduction for the Blind: A Description and Assessment," CRS Rep. RS20555.
[7] 42 U.S.C. § 12102(2).
[8] 42 U.S.C. § 706(8).
[9] 42 U.S.C. § 12210.
[10] H.Rept. 101-596, 101st Cong., 2d Sess. 64; 1990 U.S. Code Cong. & Ad. News 573.

conference report also indicates that the limitation in coverage is not intended to be narrowly construed to only persons who use drugs "on the day of, or within a matter of weeks before, the action in question."[11] The definitional section of the Rehabilitation Act was also amended to create uniformity with this definition.

Section 508 provides that an individual shall not be considered to have a disability solely because that individual is a transvestite.[12] Section 511 similarly provides that homosexuality and bisexuality are not disabilities under the Act and that the term disability does not include transvestism, transsexualism, pedophilia, exhibitionism, voyeurism, gender identity disorders not resulting from physical impairments, or other sexual behavior disorders, compulsive gambling, kleptomania, or pyromania, or psychoactive substance use disorders resulting from current illegal use of drugs.[13]

Regulatory Interpretation

The issues involving the definition of "disability" have been among the most controversial under the ADA. Although the continued validity of the regulations is questionable after the Supreme Court's recent decisions in *Sutton* and *Murphy,* the Equal Employment Opportunity Commission (EEOC) has issued regulations discussing the requirements of the definition.[14] The EEOC also issued detailed guidance on the definition on March 15, 1995 finding that the following conditions would not constitute impairments: environmental, cultural, and economic disadvantages; age; pregnancy; common personality traits; and normal deviations in height, weight and strength. However, certain aspects of these conditions could give rise to an impairment. For example, complications arising from pregnancy or conditions associated with age, such as hearing loss, could be considered to be disabilities. In addition, the guidance found that the determination of whether a condition constitutes an impairment must be made without regard to mitigating measures. The guidance also included the EEOC's interpretation of the third prong of the definition – "regarded as having a disability." This category was seen by EEOC as including individuals who

---

[11] *Id.*
[12] 42 U.S.C. §12208.
[13] 42 U.S.C. §12211.
[14] 34C.F.R. §§1630 *et seq.*

are subjected to discrimination on the basis of genetic information relating to illness, disease or other disorders.[15]
   The continuing force of the regulations and guidance is in some question after the Supreme Court's decisions in *Sutton v. United Airlines, Inc., supra,* and *Murphy v. United Parcel Service, supra.* The Court in these cases specifically held that mitigating measures such as eyeglasses or medication are relevant to the determination of whether or not a condition constitutes as impairment. In other words, the Court found that if an individual's vision is correctable by eyeglasses, that individual's visual condition would not be considered an impairment.
   Rejecting the EEOC interpretation in *Sutton,* the Supreme Court noted that no agency was given the authority to interpret the term "disability" but that because both parties accepted the regulations as valid "we have no occasion to consider what deference they are due, if any." The Court specifically noted what it considered to be conceptual difficulties with defining major life activities to include work. Similarly, in *Murphy* the Court clearly stated that its use of the EEOC regulations did not indicate that the regulations were valid. This questioning of the regulations and guidance raises issues concerning how the Court would view other agency interpretations such as those indicating that genetic discrimination would view other agency interpretations such as those indicating that genetic discrimination would be covered under the definition of individual with disability under the ADA.[16] This may be particularly important with regard to agency interpretations that rely heavily on the ADA's legislative history since the Court in *Sutton* did not consider the legislative history but found that the statutory language was sufficient to support its holding.[17]
   The EEOC has issued guidance to its field investigators to help them analyze ADA charges after the Supreme Court's decisions. This guidance emphasizes a case by case determination regarding issues of whether an individual has a disability and whether that individual is "qualified."[18] In

---

[15] *EEOC Compliance Manual,* Section 902; *BNA's Americans with Disabilities Act Manual* 70:1131. The issue of coverage of genetic disorders has been widely discussed. See CRS Report RL30006, *Genetic Information: Legal Issues Relating to Discrimination and Privacy.*

[16] EEOC Compliance Manual , Vol. 2, section 902, order 915.002,902-45 (1995).

[17] See also *Toyota Motor Manufacturing v. Williams,* 534 U.S. 184 (2002), where the Court also discussed the definition of disability and noted: "The persuasive authority of the EEOC regulations is less clear.... Because both parties accept the EEOC regulations as reasonable, we assume without deciding that they are, and we have no occasion do decide what level of deference, if any, they are due."

[18] EEOC, "Instructions for Filed Offices: Analyzing ADA Charges after Supreme Court Decisions Addressing 'Disability' and 'Qualified', (July 1999).

addition, the EEOC noted that the Supreme Court's interpretation of the ADA in *Bradgon v. Abbott, supra,* indicates that the terms "impairment," "major life activity" and "substantial limitation" are to be broadly interpreted and "the EEOC will continue to give a broad interpretation to these terms."

Supreme Court Cases

Although *Sutton* and *Murphy* were discussed briefly with regard to the EEOC's regulations, these are landmark decisions and it is critical to examine these decisions and the Supreme Court's other ADA decisions in more depth. The first ADA case to address the definitional issue was *Bragdon v. Abbott,* a case involving a dentist who refused to treat an HIV infected individual outside of a hospital.[19] In *Bragdon,* the Court found that the plaintiff's asymptomatic HIV infection was a physical impairment impacting on the major life activity of reproduction thus rending HIV infection a disability under the ADA. Two other cases the Court has decided on the definitional issue involved whether the effects of medication or assistive devices should be taken into consideration in determining whether or not an individual has a disability. The Court in the landmark decisions of *Sutton v. United Airlines, supra,* and *Murphy v. United Parcel Service, Inc, supra,* held the "determination of whether an individual is disabled should be made with reference to measures that mitigate the individual's impairment...."[20] In *Albertsons Inc. v. Kirkingburg, supra,* the Court held unanimously that the ADA does not require that an employer adopt an experimental waiver program regarding certification of an employee and stated that the ADA requires proof that the limitation on a major life activity by the impairment is substantial. Recently in *Toyota Motor Manufacturing v. Williams*[21] the Court examined what was a "substantial" limitation of a major life activity.

---

[19] 524 U.S. 624 (1998). For a more detailed discussion of this decision see CRS Report 98-599, *The Americans with Disability Act: HIV Infection is Covered Under the Act.*

[20] *Sutton v. United Airlines.* See also *Murphy v. United Parcel Service;* where the Court held that the determination of whether the petitioner's high blood pressure substantially limits one or more major life activities must be made considering the mitigating measures he employs.

[21] 534 U.S. 184 (2002).

Bragdon v. Abbott

The Supreme Court in *Bragdon v. Abbott* addressed the ADA definition of individual with a disability and held that the respondent's asymptomatic HIV infection was a physical impairment impacting on the major life activity of reproduction thus rendering the HIV infection a disability under the ADA.[22] In 1994, Dr. Bragdon performed a dental examination on Ms. Abbott and discovered a cavity. Ms. Abbott had indicated in her registration form that she was HIV positive but at that time she was asymptomatic. Dr. Bragdon told her that he would not fill her cavity in his office but would treat her only in a hospital setting. Ms. Abbott filed an ADA complaint and prevailed at the district court, courts of appeals and the Supreme Court on the issue of whether she was an individual with a disability but the case was remanded for further consideration regarding the issue of direct threat.

In arriving at its holding, Justice Kennedy, writing for the majority, first looked to whether Ms. Abbott's HIV infection was a physical impairment. Noting the immediacy with which the HIV virus begins to damage an individual's white blood cells, the Court found that asymptomatic HIV infection was a physical impairment. Second, the Court examined whether this physical impairment affected a major life activity and concluded that the HIV infection placed a substantial limitation on her ability to reproduce and to bear children and that reproduction was a major life activity. Finally, the Court examined whether the physical impairment was a substantial limitation on the major life activity of reproduction. After evaluating the medical evidence, the Court concluded that Ms. Abbott's ability to reproduce was substantially limited in two ways: (1) an attempt to conceive would impose a significant risk on Ms. Abbott's partner, and (2) an HIV infected woman risks infecting her child during gestation and childbirth.[23]

Sutton v. United Airlines and Murphy v. United Parcel Service

In *Sutton*, the Supreme Court affirmed the court of appeals decision and rejected the position of the Equal Employment Opportunities Commission (EEOC). The tenth circuit had held that United Airlines did not violate the ADA when it denied jobs to twins who had uncorrected vision of 20/200 and 20/400. Both of the twins were commercial airline pilots for regional commuter airlines and had 20/20 vision with corrective lenses. However,

---

[22] 524 U.S. 624, 118 S.Ct. 2196, 141 L.Ed. 540 (1998).

[23] Another major issue addressed in *Bragdon* involved the interoperation of the ADA's direct threat exemption which will be discussed in the section on public accommodations. For a more detailed discussion on *Bragdon* see CRS Report 98-599, *The Americans with Disabilities Act: HIV Infection is Covered Under the Act.*

United rejected their applications based on its policy of requiring uncorrected vision of 20/100 or better for its pilots. The tenth circuit noted that the twins' vision was a physical impairment but found that because it was corrected they were not substantially impaired in the major life activity of seeing. Similarly, in *Murphy* the tenth circuit relied on its ruling in *Sutton* to find that a former truck mechanic with high blood pressure was not an individual with a disability since he experiences no substantial limitations in major life activities while he takes his medication.

There are several significant implications of these decisions. Most importantly, the decisions significantly limit the reach of the definition of individual with disability. The use of mitigating factors, such as eye glasses or medication is relevant to the determination of disability. And as the *Sutton* Court stated: "a 'disability' exists only where an impairment 'substantially limits' a major life activity, not where it 'might,' 'could,' or 'would' be substantially limiting if mitigating measures were not taken." To be substantially limited in the major life activity of working was seen by the majority as being precluded from more than one type of job. The Court also emphasized that the statement of findings in the ADA that some 43,000,000 Americans have one or more physical or mental disabilities "requires the conclusion that Congress did not intend to bring under the statute's protection all those whose uncorrected conditions amount to disabilities." The proper analysis was described as examining in an individualized manner whether an individual has a disability. Thus individuals who use prosthetic limbs or a wheelchair "may be mobile and capable of functioning in society but still be disabled because of a substantial limitation on their ability to walk or run." The Court in *Sutton* and *Murphy* also observed that the third prong of the ADA's definition disability which would include individuals who are "regarded as" having a disability is relevant. The Court found that there are two ways an individual could be "regarded as" having a disability: (1) a covered entity mistakenly believes that a person has a physical impairment that substantially limits one or more major life activities, or (2) a covered entity mistakenly believes that an actual, non limiting impairment substantially limits one or more major life activities. Since the petitioners in *Sutton* did not make the argument that they were regarded as having a substantially limiting impairment, The Court did not address the issue there.

But in *Murphy* this issue was before the Court. It held that the petitioner's high blood pressure did not substantially limit him in employment since (1) he failed to demonstrate that there is a genuine issue of material fact as to whether he is regarded as disabled and (2) petitioner was able to perform a wide array of jobs.

Justices Stevens and Breyer dissented from the majority's opinion in *Sutton* and *Murphy* arguing that "in order to be faithful to the remedial purpose of the Act, we should give it a generous, rather than a miserly, construction." The dissenters found that the statutory scheme was best interpreted by looking only the existence of an impairment that substantially limits an individual either currently or in the past since "this reading avoids the counterintuitive conclusion that the ADA's safeguards vanish when individuals make themselves more employable by ascertaining ways to overcome their physical or mental limitations."

Albertsons, Inc. v. Kirkingburg

Albertsons involved a truck driver with monocular vision who alleged a violation of the ADA based on the refusal of his employer to retain him based on a waiver. The truck driver did not meet the general vision standards set by the Department of Transportation for drivers of commercial vehicles although he did qualify for a waiver. The Supreme Court in a unanimous decision held that an employer does not have to participate in an experimental waiver program.

Although the Court did not need to address definitional issues in *Albertsons,* it did so to "correct three missteps the Ninth Circuit made in its discussion of the matter." The Supreme Court found there was no question regarding the fact that the plaintiff had a physical impairment; the issue was whether his monocular vision "substantially limits" his vision. The ninth circuit had answered this question in the affirmative but the Supreme Court disagreed. First, it found that in order to be substantially limiting, a condition must impose a "significant restriction" on a major life activity, not a "difference" as determined by the ninth circuit. Second, in determining whether or not there is a disability, the individual's ability to compensate for the impairment must be taken into consideration. Third, the existence of a disability must be determined on a case-by-case basis.

Toyota Motor Manufacturing of Kentucky v. Williams

The Supreme Court in *Toyota Motor Manufacturing v. Williams*[24] examined whether the plaintiff was an individual with a disability under the first prong of the definition of individual with a disability; that is, whether she had a physical or mental impairment that substantially limits a major life activity. There was no dispute regarding the fact that the plaintiff's carpal

---

[24] 534 U.S. 184 (2002).

tunnel syndrome and tendinitis where physical impairments. The difference of opinion involved whether these impairments *substantially* limited the plaintiff in the major life activity of performing manual tasks. In order to resolve this issue, Justice O'Connor, writing for the unanimous Court, determined that the word substantial "clearly precluded impairments that interfere in only a minor way with the performance of manual tasks." Similarly, the Court found that the term "major life activity" "refers to those activities that are of central importance to daily life." Finding that these terms are to be "interpreted strictly,"[25] the Court held that "to be substantially limited in performing manual tasks, an individual must have an impairment that prevents or severely restricts the individual from doing activities that are of central importance to most people's daily lives." Significantly, the Court also stated that "[t]he impairment's impact must also be permanent or long-term." The Supreme Court's opinion emphasized the need for individualized assessment of the effect of the impairment. Justice O'Connor found it insufficient to merely submit evidence of a medical diagnosis of an impairment; rather, the individual must offer evidence that the extent of the impairment in their own situation is substantial.[26]

Generally *Williams* has been characterized as a win for employers since the Court held that the terms "major life activity" and "substantial" were to be interpreted strictly. However, one commentator has predicted that the decision will not be "a clean win for employers" since litigation will now be complicated by disputes over which life activities are affected by the disability[27].//

---

[25] Confirmation of the need for strict interpretation was found by the Court in the ADA's statement of findings and purposes where Congress stated that "some 3,000,000 Americans have one or more physical or mental disabilities." [42 U.S.C. §12101(a)(1)] Justice O'Connor observed that "if Congress had intended everyone with a physical impairment that precluded the performance of some isolated, unimportant, or particularly difficult manual task to quality as disabled, the number of disabled Americans would surely have been much higher."

[26] For a more detailed discussion of this decision see CRS Report RS21105, *The Americans with Disabilities Act: Toyota Motor Manufacturing v. Williams*, by Nancy Lee Jones.

[27] Tony Mauro, "Court's ADA Rulings Aren't Winning Kudos for Clarity," New Jersey L. J. (May 6, 2002).

Other Judicial Decisions

Numerous lower courts have addressed issues involving the definition of disability. These cases have involved such conditions as obesity,[28] cancer,[29] diabetes,[30] and multiple chemical sensitivity.[31] However, given the recent Supreme Court cases on the definition of disability, the presidential value of lower court cases decided prior to the most recent Supreme Court decisions must be carefully examined to determine if the reasoning comports with the Court's interpretation of the statute.

There have been a number of lower court cases post-*Sutton*. One of the most significant issues raised in these cases is whether an individual with a disability is required to take medication or use an assistive device to alleviate his or her condition. In a recent case involving an individual with asthma, the Maryland district court denied the ADA claim and stated: "Since plaintiff's asthma is correctable by medication and since she voluntarily refused the recommended medication, her asthma did not substantially limit her in any major life activity. A plaintiff who does not avail herself of proper treatment is not a 'qualified individual' under the ADA."[32] Other courts have focused on the other aspects of the definition concerning what is a major life activity

---

[28] The EEOC's ADA regulations state that absent unusual circumstances, "obesity is not considered a disabling impairment," 29 C.F.R. § 1630.2(j)(Appendix). See *Andrews v. Ohio*, 104 F.3d 803 (6th Cir. 1997); *Francis v. City of Meriden*, 129 F.3d 281 (2d Cir. 1997). However, several cases have found situations where obesity might by covered. See, e.g., *Cook v. Rhode Island*, 10 F.3d 17 (1st Cir. 1993); *EEOC v. Texas Bus Lines*, 923 F. Supp. 965 (S.D.Tex. 1996).

[29] In most cases, an individual with cancer would most likely be covered by the ADA since the cancer would probably limit a major life activity. But the fifth circuit court of appeals held that a woman who received radiation treatments for breast cancer was not covered since she missed very few days of work and was therefore not limited in a major life activity. *Ellison v. Software Spectrum, Inc.*, 85 F.3d 187 (5th Cir. 1996).

[30] *Lawson v. CSX Transportation Inc.*, 245 F.3d 916 (7th Cir. 2001). The Seventh Circuit held that the plaintiff's diabetes substantially limited the major life activity of eating, even with the corrective measure of taking insulin.

[31] In *Patrick. v. Southern Company Services*, 910 F.Supp. 566 (N.D.Ala. 1996), *aff'd* 103 f.3d 149 (11th Cir. 1996), the court found that alleged multiple chemical sensitivity was not a disability under the ADA since it did not substantially limit the plaintiff in the major life activity of working. However, in *Whillock v. Delta Air Lines*, 926 F. Supp. 1555 (N.S.Ga. 1995, *aff'd* 86 F.3d. 1171 (11th Cir. 1996), the court found that multiple chemical sensitivity might be a disability.

[32] *Tangires v. The Johns Hopkins Hospital*, 79 F.Supp.2d 587 (D.Md. 2000), aff'd 230 F.3d 1354 (2000). See also *Spradley v. Custom Campers, Inc.*, 68 F.Supp.2d 1225 (D.Kansas 1999). But see, *Finical v. Collections Unlimited, Inc.*, 65 F.Supp.2d 1032 (D.Ariz. 1999), where the court rejected the employer's argument that *Sutton's* individualized inquire does not permit an employer to consider the use of corrective devices which are not actually used.

and when an individual is considered to have a history of a disability or be "regarded as" having a disability.[33]

EMPLOYMENT

General Requirements

Title I of the ADA provides that no covered entity shall discriminate against a qualified individual with a disability because of the disability in regard to job application procedures, the hiring, advancement, or discharge of employees, employee compensation, job training, an other terms, conditions, and privileges of employment.[34] The term employer is defined as a person engaged in an industry affecting commerce who has 15 or more employees.[35] Therefore, the employment section of the ADA, unlike the section on public accommodations, which will be discussed subsequently, is limited in scope to employers with 15 or more employees. This parallels the coverage provided in the Civil Rights Act of 1964.

The term "employee" with respect to employment in a foreign country includes an individual who is a citizen of the United States; however, it is not unlawful for a covered entity to take action that constitutes discrimination with respect to an employee in a workplace in a foreign country if compliance would cause the covered entity to violate the law of the foreign country.[36]

If the issue raised under the ADA is employment related and the threshold issues of meeting the definition of an individual with a disability and involving an employer employing over fifteen individuals are met, the next step is to determine whether the individual is a qualified individual with a disability who, with or without reasonable accommodation, can perform the essential functions of the job.

Title I defines a "qualified individual with a disability." Such an individual is "an individual with a disability who, with or without reasonable

---

[33] For a more detailed discussion of these see CRS Report RS20432, *The Americans with Disabilities Act: Post Sutton Decisions on Definition of Disability.*

[34] 42 U.S.C. §12112(a). Recently two courts of appeal have held that this prohibition of discrimination in the "terms, conditions, or privileges of employment" creates a viable cause of action for disability-based harassment. See *Flowers v. Southern Reg'l Physical Servs., Inc.,* 247 F.3d 229 (5th Cir. 2001); *Fox v. General Motors Corp.,* 247 F.3d 169 (4th Cir. 2001).

[35] 42 U.S.C. §12111(5).

[36] P.L. 102-166 added this provision.

accommodation, can perform the essential functions of the employment position that such person holds or desires."[37] The ADA incorporates many of the concepts set forth in the regulations promulgated pursuant to section 504, including the requirement to provide reasonable accommodation unless the accommodation would pose an undue hardship on the operation of the business.[38]

"Reasonable accommodation" is defined in the ADA as including making existing facilities readily accessible to and usable by individuals with disabilities, and job restructuring, part-time or modified work schedules, reassignment to a vacant position, acquisition or modification of equipment or devices, adjustment of examinations or training materials or policies, provision of qualified readers or interpreters or other similar accommodations.[39] "Undue hardship" is defined as "an action requiring significant difficulty or expense."[40] Factors to be considered in determining whether an action would create an undue hardship include the nature and cost of the accommodation, the overall financial resources of the facility, the overall financial resources of the covered entity, and the type of operation or operations of the covered entity.

Reasonable accommodation and the related concept of undue hardship are significant concepts under the ADA and are one of the major ways in which the ADA is distinguishable from title VII jurisprudence. The statutory language paraphrased above provides some guidance for employers but the details of the requirements have been the subject of numerous judicial decisions. In addition, the EEOC issued detailed enforcement guidance on these concepts on March 1, 1999.[41] Although much of the guidance reiterates longstanding EEOC interpretations in a question and answer format, the

---

[37] 42 U.S.C. §1211(8). The EEOC has stated that a function may be essential because (1) the position exists to perform the duty, (2) there are a limited number of employees available who could perform the function, or (3) the function is highly specialized. 29 C.F.R. §1630(n)(2). A number of issues have been litigated concerning essential functions. For example, some courts have found that regular attendance is an essential function of most jobs. See e.g., *Carr v. Reno*, 23 f.3d 525 (D.C.Cir. 1994). In *Fraizier v. Simmons*, 254 F.3d 1247 (10th Cir. 2001), the tenth circuit held that a crime investigator with MS was not otherwise qualified to perform his job duties since it would be very difficult for him to stand or walk for prolonged periods, to run or to physically restrain persons. Similarly, a nurse with a back injury that prevented her from lifting more than fifteen or twenty pounds was not a qualified individual with a disability since the ability to lift fifty pounds was an essential function of her job. *Phelps v. Optima Health , Inc.*, 251 F.3d 21 (1st Cir. 2001).

[38] See 45 C.F.R. Part 84.

[39] 42 U.S.C. § 12111(9).

[40] 42 U.S.C. § 12111(10).

[41] EEOC, "EEOC Enforcement Guidance on Reasonable Accommodation and Undue Hardship Under the Americans with Disabilities Act," No. 915.002 (March 1, 1999).

EEOC also took issue with some judicial interpretations.[42] Notably the EEOC stated that

- an employee who is granted leave as a reasonable accommodation is entitled to return to his or her same position, unless this imposes an undue hardship;

- an employer is limited in the ability to question the employee's documentation of a disability ("An employer cannot ask for documentation when: (1) both the disability and the need for reasonable accommodation are obvious, or (2) the individual has already provided the employer with sufficient information to substantiate that s/he has an ADA disability and needs the reasonable accommodation requested."); and

- an employer cannot include any "quantitative, financial, or other limitations regarding the extent of the obligation to make changes to a job or work environment."

This last principle is an interesting contrast with the opinion of the seventh circuit in *Vande Zande v. State of Wisconsin Department of Administration.*[43] In *Vande Zande,* the court found that the cost of the accommodation cannot be disproportionate to the benefit. "Even if an employer is so large or wealthy – or, like the principal defendant in this case, is a state, which can raise taxes in order to finance any accommodations that it must make to disabled employees – that it may not be able to plead 'undue hardship', it would not be required to expend enormous sums in order to bring about a trivial improvement in the life of a disabled employee."[44]

---

[42] It should be emphasized that the EEOC's guidance does not have the force of regulations and courts are not bound to follow the guidance although some courts do defer to agency expertise.

[43] 44 F.3d 538 (7th Cir. 1995).

[44] *Id.* At 542-543. See also *Schmidt v. Methodist Hospital of Indiana,* 89 F.3d 342 (7th Cir. 1996), where the court found that reasonable accommodation does not require an employer to provide everything an employee requests.

Application of the Eleventh Amendment:
Garrett v. University of Alabama

On February 21, 2001, the Supreme Court decided *Garrett v. University of Alabama*.[45] In a 5-4 decision, the Court held that the Eleventh Amendment bars suits to recover monetary damages by state employees under title I of the Americans with Disabilities Act (ADA). Although the ruling is narrowly focused concerning the ADA, it has broad implications regarding federal-state power[46] and emphasizes the difficulty of drafting federal legislation under section 5 of the Fourteenth Amendment that will withstand Eleventh Amendment scrutiny.[47]

The Eleventh Amendment states: "The Judicial power of the Unites States shall not be construed to extend to any suit in law or equity, commenced or prosecuted against one of the United States by Citizens of another State, or by Citizens or Subjects of any Foreign State." The Supreme Court had found that the Eleventh Amendment cannot be abrogated by the use of Article I powers but that section 5 of the Fourteenth Amendment can be used for abrogation in certain circumstances. Section 5 of the Fourteenth Amendment states: "The Congress shall have the power to enforce, by appropriate legislation, the provisions of this article."

The circumstances where section 5 of the Fourteenth Amendment can be used to abrogate the Eleventh Amendment can be used to abrogate the Eleventh Amendment were discussed in the recent Supreme Court decisions in *College Savings Bank v. Florida Prepaid Postsecondary Educ. Expense Board*,[48] *Florida Prepaid Postsecondary Educ. Expense Board v. College Savings Bank*,[49] and *Kimely v. Florida Board of Regents*.[50] They reiterated

---

[45] For a more detailed discussion of *Garrett* see CRS Report RS20828, *University of Alabama v. Garrett: Federalism Limits on the Americans with Disability Act*.

[46] For a detailed discussion of federalism see CRS Report RL30315, *Federalism and the Constitution: Limits on Congressional Power*.

[47] It should also be observed that the Supreme Court did not address this issue in the cases it has already decided since it was not presented to the Court. "We do not address another issue presented by petitioners: whether application of the ADA to state prisons is a constitutional exercise of Congress's power under either the Commerce Clause... or §5 of the Fourteenth Amendment...." *Pennsylvania Department of Corrections v. Yeskey, supra.* "This case, as it comes to us, presents no constitutional question." *Olmstead v. L.C., supra.*

[48] 527 U.S. 666 (1999) (The Trademark Remedy Clarification Act, TRCA, which subjected states to suit for false and misleading advertising, did not validly abrogate state sovereign immunity; neither the right to be free from a business competitor's false advertising nor a more generalized right to be secure in one's business interest qualifies as a property right protected by the Due Process Clause).

[49] 527 U.S. 627 (1999)(Congress may abrogate state sovereign immunity but must do so through legislation that is appropriate within the meaning of section 5 of the Fourteenth

the principle that the Congress may abrogate state immunity from suit under the Fourteenth Amendment and found that there were conditions necessary for successful abrogation.

- Congressional power is limited to the enactment of "appropriate" legislation to enforce the substantive provisions of the Fourteenth Amendment.

- The legislation must be remedial in nature.

- There must be a "congruence and proportionality" between the injury to be prevented and the means adopted to that end.

The ADA uses both the Fourteenth Amendment and the Commerce Clause of the Constitution as its constitutional basis.[51] It also specifically abrogates state immunity under the Eleventh Amendment.[52] The ADA, then, is clear regarding its attempt to abrogate state immunity; the issue is whether the other elements of a successful abrogation are present. The Supreme Court in *Garrett* found that they were not.

Garret involved two consolidated cases brought by separate Alabama employees. One of the employees, Patricia Garrett, had been undergoing treatment for breast cancer when, she alleged, she was transferred to a lesser position after having been told that her supervisor did not like sick people. The second plaintiff, Milton Ash, alleged that the Alabama Department of Human Services did not enforce its non-smoking policy and that, therefore, he was not able to control his asthma. The Eleventh Circuit held that the state was not immune from suits for damages. The Supreme Court reversed.

Writing for the majority, Chief Justice Rehnquist briefly examined the ADA's statutory language and the general principles of the Eleventh Amendment immunity. He observed that the first step in applying these principles was to identify the scope of the constitutional right at issue, in other words, to identify constitutional rights that individuals with disabilities have to be free from discrimination. Discussing *Cleburne v. Cleburne Living*

Amendment; Congress must identify conduct that violates the Fourteenth Amendment and must tailor its legislation to remedying or preventing such conduct).

[50] 528 U.S. 62 (2000).

[51] 42 U.S.C. §12101(b)(4). The Commerce Clause would not be sufficient authority on which to abrogate state sovereign immunity since the Supreme Court's decision in *Seminole Tribe of Florida v. Florida,* 517 U.S. 44 (1996).

[52] 42 U.S.C. §12202.

Center,[53] Chief Justice Rehnquist emphasized that discrimination against individuals with disabilities is entitled to only "minimum 'rational-basis' review" and stated: "Thus, the result of *Cleburne* is that States are not required by the Fourteenth Amendment to make special accommodations for the disabled, so long as their actions towards such individuals are rational. They could quite hard headedly – and perhaps hardheartedly – hold to job qualification requirements which do not make allowance for the disabled. If special accommodations for the disabled are to be required, they have to come from positive law and not through the Equal Protection Clause."[54]

After examining the constitutional rights of individuals with disabilities, the majority opinion in *Garrett* examined whether Congress had identified a history and pattern of unconstitutional employment discrimination by the states against individuals with disabilities. Chief Justice Rehnquist observed that the authority of Congress under section 5 of the Fourteenth Amendment "is appropriately exercised only in response to state transgressions."[55] He found that the legislative history of the ADA did not identify such a pattern. Although the record was replete with examples of discrimination, Chief Justice Rehnquist noted that most of these examples were drawn from units of local government and not the states and that "the Eleventh Amendment does not extend its immunity to units of local government."[56]

The *Garrett* majority observed that even if a pattern of unconstitutional discrimination by states was found, issues to whether there was a "congruence and proportionality" between the injury to be prevented and the means adopted would raise concerns. Chief Justice Rehnquist observed that "it would be entirely rational (and therefore constitutional) for a state employer to conserve scare financial resources by hiring employees who are able to use existing facilities" but that the ADA requires that existing facilities be readily accessible to and usable by individuals with disabilities.[57] The ADA's accommodation requirements were seen as "far exceed(ing) what is constitutionally required."[58] The ADA's requirements forbidding standards, criteria, or methods of administration that disparately impact

---

[53] 473 U.S. 432 (1985). In *Cleburne*, the Supreme Court applied the Fourteenth Amendment to individuals with mental retardation and found that, although such individuals were not part of a suspect class, a zoning ordinance which group homes from certain locations violated the Fourteenth Amendment.

[54] Slip op. at 9-10.

[55] Slip op. at 10.

[56] Slip op. at 11.

[57] Slip op. at 14.

[58] Slip op. at 14.

individuals with disabilities were also seen as inconsistent with the requirements for legislation under section 5 of the Fourteenth Amendment.

In conclusion, the majority opinion states that "Congress is the final authority as to desirable public policy, but in order to authorize private individuals to recover money damages against the States, there must be a pattern of discrimination by the States which violates the Fourteenth Amendment, and the remedy imposed by Congress must be congruent and proportional to the targeted violation. Those requirements are not met here...."[59] However, after reaching this holding, the *Garrett* majority went on to note that it does not mean that individuals with disabilities have no federal recourse. The opinion was limited to the recovery of monetary damages and the standards of title I of the ADA were seen as still applicable to the states. In addition, the Court noted that the federal government could enforce those rights in action for monetary damages and that state law would offer some means of redress.

In a concurring opinion, Justice Kennedy and O'Connor, emphasized the limited nature of the opinion stating that "what is in question is not whether the Congress, acting pursuant to a power granted to it by the Constitution, can compel that States to act. What is involved in only the question whether the States can be subjected to liability in suits brought not by the Federal Government but by private persons seeking to collect moneys from the state treasury without the consent of the State."[60]

Justice Breyer, joined by Justices Stevens, Souter and Ginsburg, strongly disagreed with the majority's opinion and stated that Congress could have reasonably concluded that the title I remedies of the ADA were appropriate legislation under the Fourteenth Amendment. The emphasis in the majority opinion on the limited legislative history was described as ignoring the "powerful evidence of discriminatory treatment throughout society in general" which "implicates state governments as well, for state agencies form part of that same larger society."[61] The rules the majority used to find the legislative record inadequate were seen as flawed, using standards more appropriately applied to judges than to Congress. In the view of the dissenters, Congress has broad authority to remedy violations of the Fourteenth Amendment. "There is simply no reason to require Congress, seeking to determine facts relevant to the exercise of its §5 authority, to adopt rules or presumptions that reflect a court's institutional limitations. Unlike courts, Congress can readily gather facts from across the Nation,

---

[59] Slip op. at 16.
[60] Concurring op. at 3.
[61] Dissenting op. at 3.

assess the magnitude of a problem, and more easily find an appropriate remedy."[62]

University of Alabama v. Garrett is a major decision, further emphasizing the Court's federalism theories and raising separation of powers issues as well.[63] Although the majority does not rule out all legislation enacted pursuant to §5 of the Fourteenth Amendment, it has made the enactment of such legislation significantly less likely to withstand Eleventh Amendment scrutiny. In addition, the Court's comments on disparate impact discrimination could signal a challenge to other uses of this approach and some commentators have stated this could have implications for other statutes, including title VII of the Civil Rights Act, which prohibits racial discrimination.[64] More specifically, with regard to the ADA, the majority took pains to describe the limited nature of the holding. It is limited to title I of the ADA, deals only with monetary damages and leaves open other avenues of relief such as enforcement by the Equal Employment Opportunities Commission and state laws. However, the absence of monetary damage does make individual suits against states much less likely and has been described as a significant blow to ADA enforcement.

Several courts of appeals have examined the ADA and state sovereign immunity issues subsequent to the Supreme Court's decision in *Garrett*. The eighth circuit curt of appeals in *Gibson v. Arkansas Department of Correction,*[65] discussed *Garrett's,* language on the limited nature of its holding, and held that state officials may be sued for prospective relief under title I of the ADA. Although the state had argued that the *Garrett* discussion was mere *dicta,* the court of appeals disagreed stating: "there is no reason to think that Congress intended to limit the availability of prospective relief against states who continued to discriminate against the disabled."[66] In *Reickenbacker v. Foster*[67] the fifth circuit held that the state department of corrections was entitled to sovereign immunity with respect to mentally ill prisoners' ADA claims. The ninth circuit in *Hason v. Medical Board of California*[68] noted that the Supreme Court in *Garrett* expressly declined to

---

[62] Dissenting op. at 9.

[63] Linda Greenhouse, "The High Court's Target: Congress," *The New York Times wk3* (Feb 25, 2001.)

[64] *Id.*

[65] 265 F.3d 718 (8th Cir. 2001).

[66] See also *Grey v. Wilburn,* 270 F.3d 607 (8th Cir. 2001), where the court held that the Eleventh Amendment did not bar a claim by a securities agent with bipolar affective disorder for injunctive relief regarding registration as a securities agent.

[67] 274 F.3d 974 (5th Cir. 2001).

[68] 279 F.3d 1167 (9th Cir. 2002).

decide whether Congress had validly abrogated state sovereign immunity in enacting title II of the ADA, and held that the Eleventh Amendment did not bar a title II claim. The ninth circuit in *Demshki v. Monteith*[69] held that the ruling in *Garrett* was applicable to a claim brought under title V of the ADA regarding retaliation since the claim involved an employment issue. In addition to judicial decisions, at least one state has enacted legislation waiving its immunity for ADA purposes.[70]

The Supreme Court continues to examine federalism issues, although not in the context of the ADA. In the 2001-2002 term, the Court held in *Federal Maritime Commission v. South Carolina State Ports Authority*[71] that the states have Eleventh Amendment immunity from private lawsuits adjudicated by federal administrative agencies. The Supreme Court has also granted certiorari in *Nevada Department of Human Resources v. Hibbs,* to decide whether state employees can sue their agencies under the Family and Medical Leave Act.[72]

Other Supreme Court Employment Cases

Many of the Supreme Court decisions have involved employment situations although a number of these cases did not reach past the threshold issue of whether the individual alleging employment discrimination was an individual with a disability. There are still several significant employment issues, such as reasonable accommodations, which have not been dealt with by the Court. In addition, the landmark decision of *University of Alabama v. Garrett* on the application of the Eleventh Amendment arose in the employment context although it is discussed separately above.

---

[69] 255 F.3d 986 (9th Cir. 2001).

[70] Chapter 159, S.F.No. 1614 (Minnesota Sessions Laws, May 22, 2001). "An employee, former employee, or prospective employee of the state who is aggrieved by the state's violation of the Americans with Disabilities Act of 1990... may bring a civil action against the state in any court of competent jurisdiction for such legal or equitable relief as will effectuate the purposes of the act." This Minnesota law also waived immunity regarding the Age Discrimination in Employment Act, the Fair Labor standards Act and the Family and Medical leave Act.

[71] 122 S.Ct. 1864; 152 L.Ed.2d 962 (2002).

[72] 273 F.3d 844 (9th Cir. 2001); cert. granted, 122 S.Ct. 2618; 153 L.Ed.2d 802 (March 19, 2002).

Receipt of SSI Benefits

The relationship between receipt of SSDI benefits and the ability of an individual to pursue an ADA employment claim was the issue in *Cleveland v. Policy Management Systems Corp, supra.* The Supreme Court unanimously held that pursuit and receipt of SSDI benefits does not automatically stop a recipient from pursuing an ADA claim or even create a strong presumption against success under the ADA. Observing that the Social Security Act and the ADA both help individuals with disabilities but in different ways, the Court found that "despite the appearance of conflict that arises from the language of the two statutes, the two claims do not inherently conflict to the point where courts should apply a special negative presumption like the one applied by the Court of Appeals here." The fact that the ADA defines a qualified individual as one who can perform the essential functions of the job with or without reasonable accommodation was seen as a key distinction between the ADA and the Social Security Act. In addition, the Court observed that SSDI benefits are sometimes granted to individuals who are working.

"Qualified" Individual with a Disability

In the *Albertsons* decision discussed in part previously, the Supreme Court held that an employer need not adopt an experimental vision waiver program. Title I of the ADA prohibits discrimination in employment against a "qualified" individual with a disability. In finding that the plaintiff's inability to comply with the general regulatory vision requirements rendered him unqualified, the Court framed the question in the following manner. "Is it reasonable ... to read the ADA as requiring an employer like Albertsons to shoulder the general statutory burden to justify a job qualification that would tend to exclude the disabled, whenever the employer choose to abide by the otherwise clearly applicable, unamended substantive regulatory standard despite the Government's willingness to waive it experimentally and without any finding of its being inappropriate?" Answering this question in the negative, the Court observed that employers should not be required to "reinvent the Government's own wheel" and stated that "it is simply not credible that Congress enacted the ADA (before there was any waiver program) with the understanding that employers choosing to respect the Government's sole substantive visual acuity regulation in the face of an experimental waiver might be burdened with an obligation to defend the regulation's application according to its own terms."

In *Chevron U.S.A. Inc., v. Echazabal,*[73] The Supreme Court held unanimously that the ADA does not require an employer to hire an individual with a disability of the job in question would endanger the individual's health. The ADA's statutory language provided for a defense to an allegation of discrimination that a qualification standard is "job related and consistent with business necessity."[74] The act also allows an employer to impose as a qualification standard that the individual shall not pose a direct threat to health or safety of other individuals in the workplace[75] but does not discuss a threat to the individual's health or safety. The ninth circuit in *Echazabal* had determined that an employer violated the ADA by refusing to hire an applicant with a serious liver condition whose illness would be aggravated through exposure to the chemicals in the workplace.[76] The Supreme Court rejected the ninth circuit decision and upheld a regulation by the EEOC that allows an employer to assert a direct threat defense to an allegation of employment discrimination where the threat is posed only to the health or safety of the individual making the allegation.[77] Justice Souter found that the EEOC regulations were not the kind of workplace paternalism that the ADA seeks to outlaw. "The EEOC was certainly acting within the reasonable zone when it saw a difference between rejecting workplace paternalism and ignoring specific and documented risks to the employee himself, even if the employee would take his chances for the sake of getting a job." The Court emphasized that a direct threat defense must be based on medical judgment that uses the most current medical knowledge.

The Supreme Court had examined an analogous issue in *UAV v. Johnson Controls, Inc.,*[78] which held that under the Civil Rights Act of 1964 employers could not enforce "fetal protection" polices that kept women, whether pregnant or with the potential to become pregnant, from jobs that might endanger a developing fetus. Although this case was raised by the plaintiff, the Supreme Court distinguished the decision there from that in *Echazabal*. The *Johnson Controls* decision was described as "concerned with paternalistic judgments based on the broad category of gender, while the EEOC has required that judgments based on the direct threat provision be made on the basis of individualized risk assessments."

---

[73] 122 S.Ct. 2045; 153 L.Ed.2d 82 (2002).

[74] 42 U.S.C. §12113(a).

[75] 42 U.S.C. §12113(b).

[76] 226 F.3d 1063 (9th Cir. 2000).

[77] 29 C.F.R. §1630.15(b)(2).

[78] 499 U.S. 187 (1991).

Echazabal has been hailed by employers as "a major victory for the business community."[79] However, Andrew Imparato, the President of the American Association of People with Disabilities, stated that "The United States Supreme Court today once again demonstrated its fundamental hostility to disability rights in the workplace.... Today's decision invites paternalism and represents a major step backward for the more than 35 million working age Americans with disabilities."[80]

Collective Bargaining Agreements

The interplay between rights under the ADA and collective bargaining agreements was the subject of the Supreme Court's decision in *Wright v. Universal Maritime Service Corp., supra.* The Court held there that the general arbitration clause in a collective bargaining agreement does not require a plaintiff to use the arbitration procedure for an alleged violation of the ADA. However, the Court's decision was limited since the Court did not find it necessary to reach the issue of the validity of a union-negotiated waiver. In other words, the Court found that a general arbitration agreement in a collective bargaining agreement is not sufficient to waive rights under civil rights statutes but situations where there is a specific waiver of ADA rights were not addressed.[81]

Reasonable Accommodations and Seniority Systems

The Supreme Court in *U.S. Airways v. Barnett*[82] held that an employer's showing that a requested accommodation by an employee with a disability conflicts with the rules of a seniority system is ordinarily sufficient to establish that the requested accommodation in not "reasonable" within the meaning of the ADA. The Court, in a majority opinion by Justice Breyer, observed that a seniority system, "provides important employee benefits by creating, and fulfilling, employee expectations of fair, uniform treatment" and that to require a "typical employer to show more than the existence of a seniority system might undermine the employees' expectations of consistent, uniform treatment." Thus, in most ADA cases, the existence of a seniority system would entitle an employer to summary judgment in its favor. The

---

[79] Linda Greenhouse, "Employers, in 9-0 Ruling by Justices, Extend Winning Streak in Disabilities Act Cases," NYTA-16 (June 11, 2002).

[80] "Supreme Court Hostile to Disability Rights in the Workplace," http://www.aapd-dc.org/docs/disabilityinworkplace.htm

[81] For more information see CRS Report RL30008, *Labor and Mandatory Arbitration Agreements: Background Discussion.*

Court found no language in the ADA which would change this presumption if the seniority system was imposed by management and not by collective bargaining. However, Justice Breyer found that there were some exceptions to this rule for "special circumstances" and gave as examples situations where (1) the employer "fairly frequently" changes the seniority system unilaterally, and thereby diminishes employee expectations to the point where one more departure would "not likely make a difference" or (2) the seniority system contains so many exceptions that one more exception is unlikely to matter.

Although the majority in *Barnett* garnered five votes, the Court's views were splintered. There were strong dissents and two concurring opinions. In her concurrence, Justice O'Connor stated that she would prefer to say that the effect of a seniority system on the ADA depends on whether the seniority system is legally enforceable but that since the result would be the same in most cases as under the majority's reasoning, she joined with the majority to prevent a stalemate. The dissents took vigorous exception to the majority's decision with Justice Scalia, joined by Justice Thomas, arguing that the ADA does not permit any seniority system to be overridden. The dissent by Justice Souter, joined by Justice Ginsburg, argued that nothing in the ADA insulated seniority rules from a reasonable accommodation requirement and that the legislative history of the ADA clearly indicated congressional intent that seniority systems be a factor in reasonable accommodations determinations but not the major factor.

Employment Inquiries Relating to a Disability

Before an offer of employment is made, an employer may not ask a disability related question or require a medical examination.[83] The EEOC in its guidance on this issue stated that the rationale for this exclusion was to isolate an employer's consideration of an applicant's non-medical qualifications from any consideration of the applicant's medical condition.[84] Once an offer is made, disability related questions and medical examinations are permitted as long as all individuals who have been offered a job in that category are asked the same questions and given the same examinations.[85]

---

[82] 153 L.Ed. 2d 589; 122 S.Ct, 1516; 70 U.S.L.W. 4285 (April 29, 2002).

[83] 42 U.S.C. § 12112.

[84] EEOC, "ADA Enforcement Guidance: Preemployment Disability-Related Questions and Medical Examinations," Oct. 10, 1995.

[85] *Id.*

However, there is uncertainty concerning whether *predictive* medical testing is permissible. Some employers have tested new employees for the human immunodeficiency virus (HIV), for sickle cell traits, and for genetic markers that indicate an individual may have a higher than average susceptibility to cancer or Huntington's disease. The events of September 11, 2001 raised question concerning whether an employer may ask employees whether they will require assistance in the event of an evacuation because of a disability or medical condition. The EEOC issued a fact sheet stating that employers are allowed to ask employees to self-identify if they will require assistance because of a disability or medical conditions and providing details on how the employer may identify individuals who may require assistance.[86]

Defenses to a Charge of Discrimination

The ADA specifically lists some defenses to a charge of discrimination, including (1) that the alleged application of qualification standards has been shown to be job related and consistent with business necessity and such performance cannot be accomplished by reasonable accommodation, (2) that the term "qualification standards" can include a requirement that an individual shall not pose a direct threat to the health or safety of other individuals in the workplace,[87] and (3) that religious entities may give a preference in employment to individuals of a particular religion to perform work connected with carrying on the entities' activities.[88] In addition, religious entities may require that all applicants and employees conform to the religious tenets of the organization. The Secretary of Health and Human Services has, pursuant to a statutory requirement,[89] listed infectious diseases transmitted through the handling of food; and if the risk cannot be eliminated by reasonable accommodation, a covered entity may refuse to assign or

---

[86] [http://www.eeoc.gov/facts/evacuation.htm] For a detailed discussion of emergency procedures for employees with disabilities see Federal Emergency Management Agency, "Emergency Procedures for Employees with Disabilities in Office Occupancies."

[87] The EEOC in its regulations states that the following factors should be considered when determining whether an individual poses a direct threat: the duration of the risk, the nature and severity of the potential harm, the likelihood that the potential harm will occur, and the imminence of the potential harm. 29 C.F.R. § 1630.2(r).

[88] 42 U.S.C. § 12113.

[89] *Id.*

continue to assign an individual with such a disease to a job involving food handling.[90]

Drugs, Alcohol and Employer Conduct Rules

A controversial issue that arose during the enactment of the ADA regarding employment concerned the application of the Act to drug addicts and alcoholics. The ADA provides that, with regard to employment, *current* illegal drug users are not considered to be qualified individuals with disability. However, former drug users and alcoholics would be covered by the Act if they are able to perform the essential functions of the job. Exactly what is "current" use of illegal drugs has been the subject of some discussion. The EEOC had defined current to mean that the illegal drug use occurred "recently enough" to justify an employer's reasonable belief that drug use is an ongoing problem.[91] The courts that have examined this issue have generally found that to be covered by the ADA, the individual must be free of drugs for a considerable period of time, certainly longer than weeks.[92]

In the appendix to its regulations, EEOC further notes that "an employer, such as a law enforcement agency, may also be able to impose a qualification standard that excludes individuals with a history of illegal use of drugs if it can show that the standard is job-related and consistent with business necessity."[93] Title I also provides that a covered entity may prohibit the illegal use of drugs and the use of alcohol in the workplace.[94] Similarly, employers may hold all employees, regardless of whether or not they have a disability, to the same performance and conduct standards.[95] However, if the misconduct results from a disability, the employer must be able to demonstrate that the rule is job-related and consistent with business necessity.[96]

---

[90] 62 F.R. 49518 (Sept. 22, 1997).

[91] 29 C.F.R. Appendix §1630.3.

[92] See e.g., *Shafer v. Preston Memorial Hospital Cor,* 107 F.3d 247 (4th Cir. 1997)(Individual is a current user if he or she has illegally used drugs "in a periodic fashion during the weeks and months prior to discharge.").

[93] 29 C.F.R. Appendix §1630.3.

[94] 42 U.S.C. §12114(c); 29 C.F.R. §1630.16(b)(4).

[95] EEOC Compliance Manual §902.2(c)(4). See also *Hamilton v. Southwestern Bell Telephone Co.,* 136 F.3d 1047 (5th Cir. 1998)("the ADA does not insulate emotion or violent outbursts blamed on an impairment").

[96] EEOC Enforcement Guidance on the ADA an Psychiatric Disabilities, No. 915.002, p. 29 (March 25, 1997).

Remedies

The remedies and procedures set forth in sections 705, 706, 707, 709, and 710 of the Civil Rights Act of 1964,[97] are incorporated by reference. This provides for certain administrative enforcement as well as allowing for individual suits. The Civil Rights Act of 1991, P.L. 102-166, expanded the remedies of injunctive relief and back pay. A plaintiff who was the subject of unlawful intentional discrimination (as opposed to an employment practice that is discriminatory because of its disparate impact) may recover compensatory and punitive damages. In order to receive punitive damages, the plaintiff must show that there was discriminatory practice engaged in with malice or with reckless indifference to the rights of the aggrieved individuals. The amount that can be awarded in punitive and compensatory damages is capped, with the amounts varying from $50,000 to $300,000 depending upon the size of the business. Similarly, there is also a "good faith" exception to the award of damages with regard to reasonable accommodation.

It should also be noted that the Supreme Court addressed the issue of punitive damages in a title VII sex discrimination case, *Kolstad v. American Dental Association.*[98] The Court held in *Kolstad* that plaintiffs are not required to prove egregious conduct to be awarded punitive damages; however, the effect of this holding is limited by the Court's determination that certain steps taken by an employer may immunize them from punitive damages. Since the ADA incorporates the title VII provisions, it is likely that the holding in *Kolstad* would be applicable to ADA employment cases as well.[99]

In *Equal Employment Opportunity Commission v. Wal-mart Stores, Inc.,*[100] the tenth circuit applied *Kolstad* and affirmed an award of punitive damages under the ADA. This case involved a hearing impaired employee of Wal-mart who sometimes required the assistance of an interpreter. After being employed for about two years in the receiving department, the employee was required to attend a training session but left when the video tape shown was not close captioned and no interpreter was provided. After refusing to attend in the absence of an interpreter, the employee was transferred to the maintenance department to perform janitorial duties. When

---

[97] 42 U.S.C. §§2000e-4, 2000e-5, 2000e-6, 2000e-8, 2000e-9.

[98] 527 U.S. 526 (1999).

[99] But see *Barnes v. Gorman*, 2002 US LEXIS 4421 (June 17, 2002), where the Supreme Court held that punitive damages may not be awarded under section 202 of the ADA.

[100] 187 F.3d 1241 (10th Cir. 1999).

he questioned the transfer and asked for an interpreter, he was again denied. After threatening to file a complaint with the EEOC, the employee was suspended and later terminated from employment. He then sued and won compensatory damages and $75,000 in punitive damages. On appeal, the tenth circuit examined the reasoning in *Kolstad* and concluded that the record in *Wal-mart* "is sufficient to resolve the questions of intent and agency laid out in *Kolstad.*" With regard to intent, the court reiterated the facts and further noted that the store manager, who ultimately approved the employee's suspension, had testified that he was familiar with the ADA and its provisions regarding accommodation, discrimination and retaliation. This was seen as sufficient for a reasonable jury to conclude that Wal-mart intentionally discriminated. Wal-mart had also made an agency argument, stating that liability for punitive damages was improper because the employees who discriminated against the employee did not occupy positions of managerial control. Looking again to the reasoning in *Kolstad,* the tenth circuit noted that the Wal-mart employees had authority regarding hiring a firing decisions and observed that such authority is an indicium of supervisory or managerial capacity.

In two other cases courts drew on title VII jurisprudence to hold that the ADA allows suits for workplace harassment. In *Flowers v. Southern Regional Physician Services,*[101] the plaintiff claimed that her workplace environment and her performance reviews changed dramatically when her supervisor became aware of the plaintiff's HIV infection. She was eventually fired from her job. Although there was no precedent among the courts of appeals, the fifth circuit found that "it is evident, after a review of the ADA's language, purpose, and remedial framework, that Congress's intent in enacting the ADA was, *inter alia,* to eradicate disability-based harassment in the workplace." The Fourth Circuit in *Fox v. General Motors Corporation*[102] ruled similarly. The plaintiff in *Fox* had been on disability leave and when he returned he was placed in light duty by his doctor. He was taunted and insulted by his coworkers and supervisors and ordered to do work beyond his physical capability. In analyzing whether the ADA permits workplace harassment suits, the fourth circuit noted the parallels between the ADA and Title VII and held that "for these reasons, we have little difficulty in concluding that the ADA, like Title VII, creates a cause of action for hostile work environment harassment."

---

[101] 247 F.3d 229 (5th Cir. 2001).
[102] 247 F.3d 169 (4th Cir. 2001).

PUBLIC SERVICES

General Requirements

Title II of the ADA provides that no qualified individual with a disability shall be excluded from participation in or be denied the benefits of the services, programs, or activities of a public entity or be subjected to discrimination by any such entity.[103] "Public entity" is defined as state and local governments, any department or other instrumentality of a state or local government and certain transportation authorities. The ADA does not apply to the executive branch of the federal government; the executive branch and the U.S. Postal Service are covered by section 504 of the Rehabilitation Act of 1973.[104]

The Department of Justice regulations for title II contain a specific section on program accessibility. Each service, program, or activity conducted by a public entity, when viewed in its entirety, must be readily accessible to and usable by individuals with disabilities. However, a public entity is not required to make each of its existing facilities accessible.[105] Program accessibility is limited in certain situations involving historic preservation. In addition, in meeting the program accessibility requirement, a public entity is not required to take any action that would result in a fundamental alteration in the nature of its service, program, or activity or in undue financial and administrative burdens.[106]

Supreme Court Cases

Although title II has not been the subject of as much litigation as title I, several of the ADA cases to reach the Supreme Court have involved title II.

In the first ADA case to reach the Supreme Court, *Pennsylvania Department of Corrections v. Yeskey, supra,* the Court found in a unanimous decision that state prisons "fall squarely within the statutory definition of 'public entity'" for title II. *Yeskey* involved a prisoner who was sentenced to 18 to 36 moths in a Pennsylvania correctional facility but was recommended for placement in a motivation boot camp for first time offenders. If the boot camp was successfully completed, the prisoner would have been eligible for

---

[103] 42 U.S.C. §§12131-12133.
[104] 29 U.S.C. §794.
[105] 28 C.F.R. §35.150.
[106] *Id.*

parole in six months. The prisoner was denied admission to the program due to his medical history of hypertension and sued under the ADA. The state argued that state prisoners were not covered under the ADA since such coverage would "alter the usual constitutional balance between the States and the Federal Government." The Supreme Court rejected this argument, observing that the "ADA plainly covers state institutions *without* any exception that could cast the coverage of prisons into doubt." The Court noted that prisoners receive many services, including medical services, education and vocational programs and recreational activities so that the ADA language applying the "benefits of the services programs, or activities of a public entity" is applicable to state prisons.[107]

In *Olmstead v. Georgia, supra,* the Supreme Court examined issues raised by state mental health institutions and held that title II of the ADA requires states to place individuals with mental disabilities in community settings rather than institutions when the State's treatment professionals have determined that community placement is appropriate, community placement is not opposed by the individual with disability, and the placement can be reasonably accommodated. "Unjustified isolation... is properly regarded as discrimination based on disability groups and state governments. Although disability groups have applauded the holding that undue institutionalization qualifies as discrimination by reason of disability, the Supreme Court did place certain limitations on this right. In addition to the agreement of the individual affected, the Court also dealt with the issue of what is a reasonable modification of an existing program and stated: "Sensibly construed, the fundamental-alteration component of the reasonable-modifications regulation would allow the State to show that, in the allocation of available resources, immediate relief for the plaintiffs would be inequitable, given the responsibility the State had undertaken for the care and treatment of a large and diverse population of persons with mental disabilities." This examination of what constitutes a reasonable modification may have implications for the interpretation of similar concepts in the employment and public accommodations titles of the ADA.

---

[107] The Supreme Court had remanded this case for consideration of whether Yeskey was an individual with a disability. On remand, the district court held that he was not covered by the ADA since he was not substantially limited in a major life activity. *Yeskey v. Pennsylvania Department of Corrections,* 76 F.Supp. 2d 572 (M.D. Pa. 1999).

Other Title II Cases

In *Bartlett v. New York State Board of Law Examiners,*[108] the second circuit court of appeals held that an individual's dyslexia is a learning disability and that the New York state bar examiners were required under the ADA to make reasonable accommodations in administering the bar exam.

In another title II case, a Hawaii regulation requiring the quarantine of all dogs, including guide dogs for visually impaired individuals, was found to violate title II.[109] Another major decision under title II involved the extent to which the ADA required the modification of bar examination requirements. Other title II cases have involved whether curb ramps are required,[110] the application of title II to a city ordinance allowing open burning,[111] and the application of the ADA to a city's zoning ordinances.[112] For a discussion of Eleventh Amendment issues and title II see the preceding discussion of *Garrett supra* under title I.

Transportation Provisions

Title II also provides specific requirements for public transportation by intercity and commuter rail and for public transportation other than by aircraft or certain rail operations.[113]

All new vehicles purchased or leased by a public entity that operates a fixed route system must be accessible, and good faith efforts must be

---

[108] 156 F.3d 321 (2d Cir. 1998), vacated and remanded for further consideration in light of *Sutton, Murphy and Albertsons,* 527 U.S. 1031 (1991). The second circuit held that plaintiff may be disabled, 226 F.3d 69 (2d Cir. 2000), petition for certiorari filed, March 21, 2001.

[109] *Crowder v. Kitagawa,* 81 F. 3d 1480 (9th Cir. 1996). The court stated: "Although Hawaii's quarantine requirement applies equally to all persons entering the state with a dog, its enforcement burdens visually-impaired persons in a manner different than and greater than it burdens others. Because of the unique dependence upon guide dogs among many of the visually-impaired, Hawaii's quarantine effectively denies these persons.... meaningful access to state services, programs, and activities while such services, programs, and activities remain open and easily accessible by others."

[110] In *Kinney v. Yerusalim,* 812 F.Supp. 547 (E.D. Pa. 1993), *aff'd* 9 F.3d 1067 (3d Cir. 1993), *cert. den.,* 511 U.S. 1033, 128 L.Ed.2d 196, 114 S.Ct. 1545 (1994), the court found that street repair projects must include curb ramps for individuals with disabilities. See also 28 C.F.R. §35.151(e)(1), where the Department of Justice detailed the requirements for curb ramps.

[111] *Heather K.v. City of Mallard, Iowa,* 946 F.Supp. 1373 (N.D.Iowa 1996).

[112] *Innovative Health Systems, Inc. v. City of White Plains,* 117 F.3d 37 (2d Cir. 1997).

demonstrated with regard to the purchase or lease of accessible use vehicles. Retrofitting of existing buses is not required. Paratransit services must be provided by a public entity that operates a fixed route service, other than one providing solely commuter bus service.[114] Rail systems must have at least one car per train that is accessible to individuals with disabilities.[115]

Remedies

The enforcement remedies of section 505 of the Rehabilitation Act of 1973, 29 U.S.C. §794a, are incorporated by reference.[116] These remedies are similar to those of title VI of the Civil Rights Act of 1964, and include damages and injunctive relief. The Attorney General had promulgated regulations relating to subpart A of the title,[117] and the Secretary of Transportation has issued regulations regarding transportation.[118]

Barnes v. Gorman

The Supreme Court in *Barnes v. Gorman*[119] held in a unanimous decision that punitive damages may not be awarded under section 202[120] of the ADA and section 504 of the Rehabilitation Act of 1973.[121] Jeffrey Gorman uses a wheelchair and lacks voluntary control over his lower torso which necessitates the use of a catheter attached to a urine bag. He was arrested in 1992 after fighting with a bouncer at a nightclub and during his transport to the police station suffered significant injuries due to the manner in which he was transported. He sued the Kansas City police and was awarded over $1 million in compensatory damages and $1.2 million in punitive damages. The eighth circuit court of appeals upheld the award of

---

[113] 42 U.S.C. §§12141-12165. P.L. 104-287 added a new definition. The term "commuter rail transportation" has the meaning given the term "commuter rail passenger transportation" in 45 U.S.C. §502(9).

[114] 42 U.S.C. §12143.

[115] 42 U.S.C. §12162.

[116] 42 U.S.C. §12133.

[117] 28 C.F.R. Part 35.

[118] 49 C.F.R. Parts 27, 37, 38.

[119] 122 S.Ct. 2057; 153 L.Ed.2d 230 (2002).

[120] 42 U.S.C. §12132. Section 203, 42 U.S.C. §12133, contains the enforcement provisions.

[121] 29 U.S.C. §794. Section 504 in relevant part prohibits discrimination against individuals with disability in any program or activity that receives federal financial assistance. The requirements of section 504, its regulations, and judicial decisions were the model for the statutory language in the ADA where the nondiscrimination provisions are not limited to entities that received federal financial assistance,

punitive damages but the Supreme Court reversed. Although the Court was unanimous in the result, there were two concurring opinions and the concurring opinion by Justice Stevens, joined by Justices Ginsburg and Breyer, disagreed with the reasoning used in Justice Scalia's opinion for the Court.

Justice Scalia observed that the remedies for violations of both section 202 of the ADA and section 504 of the Rehabilitation Act are "coextensive with the remedies available in a private cause of action brought under title VI of the Civil Rights Act of 1964."[122] Neither section 504 nor title II of the ADA specifically mention punitive damages, rather they reference the remedies of title VI of the Civil Rights Act. Title VI is based on the congressional power under the Spending Clause[123] to place conditions on grants. Justice Scalia noted that Spending Clause legislation is "much in the nature of a contract" and, in order to be a legitimate use of this power, the recipient must voluntarily and knowingly accept the terms of the "contract." "If Congress intends to impose a condition on the grant of federal moneys, it must do so unambiguously."[124] This contract law analogy was also found to be applicable to determining the scope of the damages remedies and, since punitive damages are generally not found to be available for a breach of contract, Justice Scalia found that they were not available under title VI, section 504 or the ADA.

PUBLIC ACCOMMODATIONS

Statutory Requirements

Title III provides that no individual shall be discriminated against on the basis of disability in the full and equal enjoyment of the goods, services, facilities, privileges, advantages, or accommodations of any place of public accommodation by any person who owns, leases (or leases to), or operates a place of public accommodation.[125] Entities that are covered by the term "public accommodation" are listed, and include, among others, hotels, restaurants, theaters, auditoriums, laundromats, museums, parks, zoos, private schools, day care centers, professional offices of health care

---

[122] 42 U.S.C. §2000d *et seq.*
[123] U.S. Const., Art. I§8, cl. 1.
[124] *Pennhurst State School and Hospital v. Halderman,* 4512 U.S. 1, 17 (1981).
[125] 42 U.S.C. §12182.

providers, and gymnasiums.[126] Religious institutions or entities controlled by religious institutions are not included on the list.

There are some limitations on the nondiscrimination requirements, and a failure to remove architectural barriers is not a violation unless such a removal is "readily achievable."[127] "Readily achievable" is defined as meaning "easily accomplishable and able to be carried out without much difficulty or expense."[128] Reasonable modifications in practices, policies or procedures are required unless they would fundamentally alter the nature of the goods, services, facilities, or privileges or they would result in an undue burden.[129] An undue burden is defined as an action involving "significant difficulty or expense."[130]

Title III contains a specific exemption for religious entities.[131] This applies when an entity is controlled by a religious entity. For example, a preschool that is run by a religious entity would not be covered under the ADA; however a preschool that is not run by a religious entity but that rents space from the religious entity, would be covered by title III.

Similarly, title III does not apply to private clubs or establishments exempted from coverage under title II of the Civil Rights Act of 1964.[132] In interpreting this provision,[133] the Department of Justice has noted that courts have been most inclined to find private club status in cases where (1) members exercise a high degree of control over club operations, (2) the membership selection process is highly selective, (3) substantial membership fees are charged, (4) the entity is operated on a nonprofit basis, and (5) the club was not founded specifically to avoid compliance with federal civil rights law. Facilities of a private club lose their exemption, however, to the extent that they are made available for use by nonmembers as places of public accommodation.[134]

Title III also contains provisions relating to the prohibition of discrimination in public transportation services provided by private entities.

---

[126] 42 U.S.C. §12181.
[127] 42 U.S.C. §12182(b)(2)(A)(iv).
[128] 42 U.S.C. §12181.
[129] 42 U.S.C. §12182(b)(2)(A).
[130] 28 C.F.R. §36.104.
[131] 42 U.S.C. §12187.
[132] 42 U.S.C. §2000a-3(a).
[133] 42 U.S.C. 12187.
[134] Department of Justice, "ADA Title III Technical Assistance Manual" III-1.6000.

Purchases of over-the-road buses are to be made in accordance with regulations issued by the Secretary of Transportation.[135]

Supreme Court Cases

The nondiscrimination mandate of title III does not require that an entity permit an individual to participate in or benefit from the services of a public accommodation where such an individual poses a direct threat to the health or safety of others. This issue was discussed by the Supreme Court in *Bragdon v. Abbott, supra,* where the Court stated that "the existence, or nonexistence, of a significant risk must be determined from the standpoint of the person who refuses the treatment or accommodation, and the risk assessment must be based on medical or other objective evidence." Dr. Bragdon had the duty to assess the risk of infection "based on the objective, scientific information available to him and other in his profession. His belief that a significant risk existed, even if maintained in good faith, would not relieve him from liability." The Supreme Court remanded the case for further consideration of the direct threat issue. On remand, the first circuit court of appeals held that summary judgment was warranted finding that Dr. Bragdon's evidence was too speculative or too tangential to create a genuine issue of fact.[136]

The Supreme Court declined to review a fourth circuit of appeals decision regarding the direct threat exception to title III. In *Montalvo v. Radcliffe,*[137] the fourth circuit held that excluding a child who has HIV from karate classes did not violate the ADA because the child posed a significant risk to the health and safety of others which could not be eliminated by reasonable modification.

Martin v PGA Tour and "Fundamental Alteration"

In *Martin v. PGA Tour,* the Supreme Court in a 7-2 decision by Justice Stevens held that the ADA's requirements for equal access gave a golfer with a mobility impairment the right to use a golf cart in professional

---

[135] 42 U.S.C. §12184. This section was amended by P.L. 104-59 to provide that accessibility requirements for private over-the-road buses must be met by small providers within three years after the issuance of final regulations and with respect to other providers, within two years after the issuance of such regulations.

[136] *Abbott v. Bragdon,* 163 F.3d 87 (1st Cir. 1998), *cert. den.,* 526 U.S. 1131(1999).

[137] 167 F.3d 873 (4th Cir. 1999), *cert. denied,* 528 U.S. 813 (1999).

competitions.[138] The ninth circuit had ruled that the use of the cart was permissible since it did not "fundamentally alter" the nature of the competition.[139]

Title III of the ADA defines the term "public accommodation," specifically listing golf courses.[140] The Majority opinion looked at this definition and the general intent of the ADA to find that golf tours and their qualifying rounds "fit comfortably within the coverage of title III." The Court then discussed whether there was a violation of the substantive nondiscrimination provision of Title III. The ADA states that discrimination includes "a failure to make reasonable modifications in policies, practices, or procedures, when such modifications are necessary to afford such goods, services, facilities, privileges, advantages, or accommodations to individuals with disabilities, unless the entity can demonstrate that making such modifications would *fundamentally alter the nature of such goods, services, facilities, privileges, advantages, or accommodations*."[141]

In theory, the Court opined, there might be a fundamental alteration of a golf tournament in two ways: (1) an alteration in an essential aspect of the game, such as changing the diameter of the hole, might be unacceptable even

---

[138] 532 U.S. 661 (2001).

[139] 204 F.3d 994 (9th Cir. 2000).

[140] 42 U.S.C. §12181(7).

[141] 42 U.S.C. §12182(b)(2)(A)(ii)(emphasis added). The Department of Justice regulations echo the statutory language and provide the following illustration. "A health car provider may refer individual with a disability to another provider if that individual is seeking, or requires, treatment or services outside of the referring provider's area of specialization, and if the referring provider would make a similar referral for an individual without a disability who seeks or requires the same treatment or services." 28 C.F.R. §36.302. The concept of fundamental alteration did not originate in the statutory language of the ADA but was derived from Supreme Court interpretation of section 504 of the Rehabilitation Act of 1973, 29 U.S.C. §794, which, in part, prohibits discrimination against an individual with a disability in any program or activity that receives federal financial assistance and was the model on which the ADA was based. In *Southeastern Community College v. Davis*, 442 U.S. 397 (1979), the Supreme Court addressed a suit by a hearing impaired woman who wished to attend a college nursing program. The college rejected her application because it believed her hearing disability made it impossible for her to participate safely in the normal clinical training program and to provide safe patient care. The supreme Court found no violation of section 505 and held that it did "not encompass the kind of curricular changes that would be necessity to accommodate respondent in the nursing program." Since Davis could not function in clinical courses without close supervision, the Court further observed that "whatever benefits respondent might realize from such a course of study, she would not receive even a rough equivalent of the training a nursing program normally gives. Such a fundamental alteration in the nature of a program is far more than the 'modification' the regulation requires." (At 409-410) In conclusion, the Court found that "nothing in the language or history of § 504 reflects an intention to limit the freedom of an educational institution to require reasonable physical qualifications for admission to a clinical training program." (At 414).

if it affected all players equally, or (2) a less significant change that only a peripheral impact on the game might give a golfer with a disability an advantage over others and therefore fundamentally alter the rules of competition. Looking at both these types of situations, Justice Stevens found that a waiver of the walking rule for Casey Martin did not amount to a fundamental alteration. He noted that the essence of the game was shot-making and that the walking rule was not an indispensable feature of tournament golf as golf carts are allowed on the Senior PGA Tour as well as certain qualifying events. In addition, Justice Stevens found that the fatigue from walking the approximately five miles over five hours was not significant. Regarding the question of whether allowing Casely Martin to use a cart would give him an advantage, the majority observed that an individualized inquiry must be made concerning whether a specific modification for a particular person's disability would be reasonable under the circumstances and yet not be a fundamental alteration. In examining the situation presented, the majority found that Casey Martin endured greater fatigue even with a cart than other contenders do by walking.

Justice Scalia, joined by Justice Thomas, wrote a scathing dissent describing the majority's opinion as distorting the text of Title III, the structure of the ADA and common sense. The dissenters contended that title III of the ADA applies only to particular places and persons and does not extend to golf tournaments. The dissent also contended that "the rules are the rules," that they are by nature arbitrary, and there is no basis for determining any of them "non-essential."

ADA and the Internet

On November 2, 1999, the National Federation of the Blind (NFB) filed a complaint against America Online (AOL) in federal district court alleging that AOL violated title III of the ADA.[142] NFB and other blind plaintiffs stated that they could only independently use computers by concurrently

---

[142]It should be noted that section 508 of the Rehabilitation Act of 1973, 29 U.S.C. §794(d), as amended by P.L. 105-220, requires that the electronic and information technology used by federal agencies be accessible to individuals with disabilities, including employees and members of the public. On December 21, 2000 the Architectural and Transportation Barriers Compliance Board (Access Board) issued standards providing technical criteria specific to various types of technologies and performance-based requirements. 65 Fed. Reg. 80500 (Dec. 21, 2000). To be published at 36 C.F.R. Part 1194. On January 22, 2001, the Federal Acquisition Regulations (FAR) Council published a proposed rule to implement section 508. [http://www.access-board.gov/sec508/FARnotice.htm.] To be published at 48 C.F.R. Parts 2, 7, 10, 11, 12, and 39.

running screen access software programs for the blind that covert visual information into synthesized speech or braille. They alleged that AOL had designed its service so that it is incompatible with screen access software programs for the blind, failing "to remove communications barriers presented by its designs thus denying the blind independent access to this service, in violation of Title III of the ADA, 42 U.S.C. §12181, et seq."[143] This complaint attracted wide spread interest since the implications are significant. The case was settled on July 26, 2000.[144]

One of the relevant issues in resolving this novel problem is whether a place of public accommodation is limited to actual physical structures. The first circuit court of appeals has held that public accommodations are not so limited, reasoning that "to exclude this broad category of businesses from the reach of Title III and limit the application of Title III to physical structures which persons must enter to obtain goods and services would run afoul of the purpose of the ADA."[145] The seventh circuit in *Doe v. Mutual of Omaha Insurance Company*[146] agreed with the first circuit. In *Doe* judge Posner discussed the nondiscrimination requirements of title III in the context of a case involving a cap on insurance policies for AIDS and AIDS related complications and found that "The core meaning of this provision, plainly enough, is that the owner or operator of a store, hotel, restaurant, dentist's office, travel agency, theater, Web site, or other facility (whether in physical space or in electronic space) ... that is open to the public cannot exclude disabled persons from entering the facility, and, once in, from using facility in the same way that the nondisabled do."[147] The court reasoned the "the owner or operator of, say, a camera store can neither bar the door to the disabled nor let them in but then refuse to sell its cameras to them on the same terms as to other customers."[148] However, Judge Posner found no violation of the ADA in this case and concluded that "section 302(a) does not require a seller to alter his product to make it equally valuable to the disabled and nondisabled...."[149]

---

[143] *National Federation of the Blind v. America Online*, Complaint, [http://www.nfb.org./aol compl.htm.] (Nov. 2, 1999).

[144] The settlement agreement can be found at the National Federation of the Blind website, [http://www.nfb.org.]

[145] *Carparts Discrimination Center, Inc. v. Automotive Wholesalers' Association of New England, Inc.*, 37 F.3d 12 (1st Cir. 1994).

[146] 179 F.3d 557 (7th Cir. 1999), *cert. denied*, 528 U.S. 1106 (2000).

[147] *Id.* at 559 (emphasis added.)

[148] *Id.*

[149] *Id.* at 563.

Most recently, the second circuit joined the first and seventh circuits in finding that the ADA is not limited to physical access. In *Pallozzi v. Allstate Life Insurance Co.,*[150] the court stated that "Title III's mandate that the disabled be accorded 'full and equal enjoyment of goods, [and] services... of any place of public accommodation,' suggest to us that the statute was meant to guarantee them more than mere physical access."

On the other hand, the third, sixth and ninth circuits apparently restrict the concept of public accommodations to physical places. In *Stoutenborough v. National Football League, Inc.,*[151] the sixth circuit dealt with a case brought by an association of individuals with hearing impairments who filed suit against the National Footbal League (NFL) and several television stations under title III alleging that the NFL's blackout rule discriminated against them since they had no other way of accessing football games when live telecasts are prohibited. The sixth circuit rejected this allegation holding that the prohibitions of title III are restricted to places of public accommodations. Similarly, in *Parker v. Metropolitan Life Insurance Co.*[152] the sixth circuit held that the ADA's nondiscrimination prohibition relating to public accommodations did not prohibit an employer from providing employees disabled by physical illness than those disabled by mental illness. In arriving at this holding, the sixth circuit found that "a benefit plan offered by an employer is not a good offered by a place of public accommodation.... A public accommodation is a physical place."[153]

In *Ford v. Schering-Plough Corporation,*[154] the third circuit found a disparity in benefits for physical and mental illnesses did not violate the ADA and found that the disability benefits at issue did not fall within title III. The court stated "This is keeping with the host of examples of public accommodations provided by the ADA, all of which refer to places."[155] This conclusion was found to be in keeping with judicial decisions under title II of the Civil Rights Act of 1964, 42 U.S.C. §2000(a).

Another issue under title III is whether franchisers are subject to the title. In *Nef v. American Dairy Queen Corp.,* the fifth circuit court of appeals found that a franchiser with limited control over the store a franchisee runs is not covered under title III of the ADA.[156]

---

[150] 198 F.3d 28 (2d Cir. 1999).
[151] 59 F.3d 580 (6th Cir. 1995), *cert. denied,* 516 U.S. 1028 (1995).
[152] 121 F.3d 1006 (6th Cir. 1997), *cert. denied,* 522 U.S. 1084 (1998).
[153] *Id.* At 1010. See also, *Lenox v. Healthwise of Kentucky,* 149 F.3d 453 (6th Cir. 1999).
[154] 145 F.3d 601 (3d Cir. 1998), *cert. denied,* 525 U.S. 1093 (1999).
[155] *Id.* At 612.
[156] 58 F.3d 1063 (5th Cir. 1995), *cert. den.,* 516 U.S. 1045 (1996).

Remedies

The remedies and procedures of title II of the Civil Rights Act of 1964 are incorporated in title III of the ADA. Title II of the Civil Rights Act has generally been interpreted to include injunctive relief, not damages. In addition, state and local governments can apply to the Attorney General to certify that state or local building codes meet or exceed the minimum accessibility requirements of the ADA. The Attorney General may bring pattern or practice suits with a maximum civil penalty of $50,000 for the first violation and $100,000 for a violation in a subsequent case. The monetary damages sought by the Attorney General do not include punitive damages. Courts may also consider an entity's "good faith" efforts in considering the amount of the civil penalty. Factors to be considered in determining good faith include whether an entity could have reasonably anticipated the need for an appropriate type of auxiliary aid to accommodate the unique needs of a particular individual with a disability. Regulations relating to public accommodations have been promulgated by the Department of Justice[157] and regulations relating to the transportation provisions of title III have promulgated by the Department of Transportation.[158]

TELECOMMUNICATIONS

Title IV of the ADA amends title II of the Communications Act of 1934[159] by adding a section providing that the Federal Communication shall ensure that interstate and intrastate telecommunications relay services are available, to the extent possible and in the most efficient manner, to hearing impaired and speech impaired individuals. Any television public services announcement that is produced or funded in whole or part by any agency or instrumentality of the federal government shall include closed captioning of the verbal content of the announcement. The FCC is given enforcement authority with certain exceptions.[160]

---

[157]28 C.F.R. Part 36.
[158]49 C.F.R. Parts 27, 37, 38.
[159]47 U.S.C. §§201 et seq.
[160]47 U.S.C. §255.

MISCELLANEOUS PROVISIONS IN TITLE V

Title V contains an amalgam of provisions, several of which generated considerable controversy during ADA debate. Section 501 concerns the relationship of the ADA to other statutes and bodies of law. Subpart (a) states that "except as otherwise provided in this Act, nothing in the Act shall be construed to apply a lesser standard than the standards applied under title V of the Rehabilitation Act ... or the regulations issued by Federal agencies pursuant to such title." Subpart (b) provides that nothing in the Act shall be construed to invalidate or limit the remedies, rights and procedures of any federal, state or local law that provides greater or equal protection. Nothing in the Act is to be construed to preclude the prohibition of or restrictions on smoking. Subpart (d) provides that the Act does not require an individual with a disability to accept an accommodation which that individual chooses not to accept.[161]

Subpart (c) of section 501 limits the application of the Act with respect to the coverage of insurance; however, the subsection may not be used as a subterfuge to evade the purposes of titles I and II. The exact parameters of insurance coverage under the ADA are somewhat uncertain. As the EEOC has stated: "the interplay between the nondiscrimination principles of the ADA and employer provided health insurance, which is predicated in the ability to make health-related distinctions, is both unique and complex."[162] The eighth circuit of appeals in *Henderson v. Bodine Aluminum, Inc.* issued a preliminary injection compelling the plaintiff's employer to pay for chemotherapy that required an autologous bone marrow transplant.[163] The plaintiff was diagnosed with an aggressive form of breast cancer and her oncologist recommended entry into a clinical trial that randomly assigns half of its participants to high dose chemotherapy that necessitates an autologous bone marrow transplant. Because of the possibility that the plaintiff might have the more expensive bone marrow treatment, the employer's health plan refused to precertify the placement noting that the policy covered high dose chemotherapy only for certain types of cancer, not breast cancer. The court concluded that, "if the evidence shows that a given treatment is non-experimental – that is, if it is widespread, safe, and a significant

---

[161]29 U.S.C. §§790 *et seq.*
[162]EEOC, "Interim Policy Guidance on ADA and Health Insurance," BNA's Americans with Disabilities Act Manual 70:1051 (June 8, 1993). This guidance deals solely with the ADA implications of disability-based health insurance plan distinctions and states that "insurance distinctions that are not based on disability, and that are applied equally to all insured employees, do not discriminate on the basis of disability and so do not violate the ADA."
[163]70 F.3d 958 (8th Cir. 1995).

improvement on traditional therapies – and the plan provides the treatment for other conditions directly comparable to the one at issue, the denial of treatment violates the ADA."[164]

Section 502 abrogates the Eleventh Amendment state immunity from suit and was discussed in the section on public services. Section 503 prohibits retaliation and coercion against an individual who has opposed an act or practice made unlawful by the ADA. Section 504 requires the Architectural and Transportation Barriers Compliance Board (ATBCB) to issue guidelines regarding accessibility. Section 505 provides for attorney's fees in "any action or administrative proceeding" under the Act. Section 506 provides for technical assistance to help entities covered by the Act in understanding their responsibilities. Section 507 provides for a study by the National Council on Disability regarding wilderness designations and wilderness land management practices and "reaffirms" that nothing in Wilderness Act is to be construed as prohibiting the use of a wheelchair in a wilderness area by an individual whose disability requires the use of wheelchair. Section 513 provides that "where appropriate and to the extent authorized by law, the use of alternative means of dispute resolution ... is encouraged ...."[165] Section 514 provides for severability of any provision of the Act that is found to be unconstitutional.

The coverage of Congress was a major controversy during the House-Senate conference on the ADA. Although the original language of the ADA did provide for some coverage of the legislative branch, congress expanded upon this in the Congressional Accountability Act, P.L. 104-1. The major area of expansion was the incorporation of remedies that were analogous to those in the ADA applicable to the private sector.[166]

---

[164]See also *Rogers v. Department of Health and Environmental Control*, 174 F.3d 431 (4th Cir. 1999), were the fourth circuit court of appeals held that the ADA does not require employers to offer the same long-term disability insurance benefits for mental and physical disabilities.

[165]42 U.S.C. §12212.

[166]For a more detailed discussion of the application of the ADA to Congress see CRS Report 95-557, *Congressional Accountability Act of 1995*. Congress has also applied the employment and public accommodation provisions of the ADA to the Executive Offece of the President. P.L. 104-331 (October 26, 1996).

Chapter 12

THE AMERICANS WITH DISABILITIES ACT (ADA): SUPREME COURT DECISIONS

Nancy Lee Jones

INTRODUCTION

Eleven years after enactment of Americans with Disabilities Act (ADA), 42 U.S.C. §§12101 *et seq.,* the Supreme Court has decided nine cases on the act. These decisions will have a broad impact on ADA interpretation. In the most recent Supreme Court decision, *University of Alabama v. Garrett,* decided February 21, 2001, the Court held that the Eleventh Amendment bars suits to recover monetary damages by state employees under title I of the ADA, a case that has significant implications regarding federal-state relations. This chapter will provide a brief analysis of the Supreme Court's decisions and will be updated as appropriate.

BACKGROUND

The Americans with Disabilities Act, 42 U.S.C. §§12101, *et seq.,* provides broad nondiscrimination protection for individuals with disabilities in employment, public services, public accommodations and services operated by private entities, and transportation, telecommunications providers. Enacted in 1990, the ADA is a civil rights statute that has as its purpose "to provide a clear and comprehensive national mandate for the elimination of discrimination against individuals with disabilities."[1] It has been the subject of numerous lower court decisions which are just beginning to reach the Supreme Court. Since 1998, the Supreme Court decided nine ADA cases, most recently *University of Alabama v. Garrett.*[2] The Court has heard oral argument and has pending *Martin v. PGA Tour,*[3] concerning the interpretation of the concept of fundamental alteration in title III of the ADA. Recently, the Court granted *certiorari in Toyota Motor Manufacturing of Kentucky v. Williams*[4] and *U.S. Airways v. Barnett.*[5]

DEFINITION OF DISABILITY

The threshold issue in any ADA case is whether the individual alleging discrimination is an individual with a disability. The ADA defines the term disability with respect to an individual as "(A) a physical or mental impairment that substantially limits one or more of the major life activities of such individual; (B) a record of such an impairment; or (C) being regarded as having such an impairment."[6] The first ADA case to address this issue was *Bragdon v. Abbott,* a case involving a dentist who refused to treat an HIV infected individual outside of a hospital.[7] In *Bragdon,* the Court found that the plaintiff's asymptomatic HIV infection was a physical impairment impacting on the major life activity of reproduction thus rending HIV infection a disability under the ADA. Two other cases the Court has decided on the definitional issue involved whether the effects of medication or assistive devices should be taken into consideration in determining whether

---

[1] 42 U.S.C. § 12102(b)(1).

[2] 531 U.S. 356 (2001).

[3] 204 F.3d 994 (9th Cir. 2000), *cert. granted,* 530 U.S. 1306 (2000).

[4] 224 F.3d 840 (6th Cir. 2000), *cert. granted,* 69 U.S.L.W. 3670 (April 16, 2001). The issue presented is whether an impairment that precluded an individual from performing only a limited number of tasks associated with a specific job qualifies the individual for ADA coverage.

[5] 228 F.3d 1105 (9th Cir. 2000), *cert. granted,* 69 U.S.L.W. 3670 (April 16, 2001). *Barnett* presents the issue of whether under title I a seniority system is an automatic bar to reassignment or whether the seniority system may be used as a factor in an undue hardship analysis.

[6] 42 U.S.C. §12102.

[7] 524 U.S. 624 (1998). For a more detailed discussion of this decision see CRS Report 98-599, *The Americans with Disabilities Act: HIV Infection is Covered Under the Act,* by Nancy Lee Jones.

or not an individual has a disability. The Court in the landmark decision of *Sutton v. United Air Lines*[8] and in *Murphy v. United Parcel Service, Inc,*[9] held the "determination of whether an individual is disabled should be made with reference to measures that mitigate the individual's impairment...."[10] Finally, in *Albertsons Inc. v. Kirkingburg*[11] the Court held unanimously that the ADA requires proof that the limitation on a major life activity by the impairment is substantial.

In *Sutton,* the Supreme Court affirmed the court of appeals decision and rejected the position of the Equal Employment Opportunities Commission (EEOC). The tenth circuit had held that United Airlines did not violate the ADA when it denied jobs to twins who had uncorrected vision of 20/200 and 20/400. Both of the twins were commercial airline pilots for regional commuter airlines and had 20/20 vision with corrective lenses. However, United rejected their applications based on its policy of requiring uncorrected vision of 20/100 or better for its pilots. The tenth circuit noted that the twins' vision was a physical impairment but found that because it was corrected, they were not substantially impaired in the major life activity of seeing. Similarly, in *Murphy* the tenth circuit relied on its ruling in *Sutton* to find that a former truck mechanic with high blood pressure was not an individual with a disability since he experiences no substantial limitations in major life activities while he takes his medication.

There are several significant implications of these decisions. Most importantly, the decisions limit the reach of the definition of individual with disability. As the *Sutton* Court stated: "a 'disability' exists only where an impairment 'substantially limits' a major life activity, not where it 'might,' 'could,' or 'would' be substantially limiting if mitigating measures were not taken." To be substantially limited in the major life activity of working was seen by the majority as being precluded from more than one type of job. The Court also emphasized that the statement of findings in the ADA that some 43,000,000 Americans have one or more physical or mental disabilities "requires the conclusion that Congress did not intend to bring under the statute's protection all those whose uncorrected conditions amount to disabilities." The proper analysis was described as examining in an individualized manner whether an individual has a disability. Thus

---

[8] 527 U.S. 471 (1999).
[9] 527 U.S. 516 (1999).
[10] *Sutton v. United Airlines.* See also *Murphy v. United Parcel Service,* where the Court held that the determination of whether the petitioner's high blood pressure substantially limits one or more major life activities must be made considering the mitigating measures he employs.
[11] 527 U.S. 555 (1999).

individuals who use prosthetic limbs or wheelchair "may be mobile and capable of functioning in society but still be disabled because of a substantial limitation on their ability to walk or run." The Court in *Sutton* and *Murphy* also observed that the third prong of the ADA's definition of disability which would include individuals who are "regarded as" having a disability is relevant. The Court found that there are two ways an individual could be "regarded as" having a disability: (1) a covered entity mistakenly believes that a person has a physical impairment that substantially limits one or more major life activities, or (2) a covered entity mistakenly believes that an actual, nonlimiting impairment substantially limits one or more major life activities. Since the petitioners in *Sutton* did not make the argument that they were regarded as having a substantially limiting impairment, the Court did not address the issue there. But in *Murphy* this issue was before the Court. It held that the petitioner's high blood pressure did not substantially limit him in employment since (1) he failed to demonstrate that there is a genuine issue of material fact as to whether he is regarded as disabled and (2) petitioner was able to perform a wide array of jobs.

Another significant aspect to the Court's decisions was the comments on the EEOC regulations. The EEOC had taken the position that whether or not an individual has a disability should be determined by what his or her condition would be without medication or an assistive device. Rejecting this EEOC interpretation, in *Sutton* the Supreme Court noted that no agency was given the authority to interpret the term "disability" but that because both parties accepted the regulations as valid "we have no occasion to consider what deference they are due, if any." The Court specifically noted what it considered to be conceptual difficulties with defining major life activities to include work. Similarly, in *Murphy* the Court clearly stated that its use of the EEOC regulations did not indicate that the regulations were valid. This questioning of the regulations and guidance raises issues concerning how the Court would view other agency interpretations such as those indicating that genetic discrimination would be covered under the ADA.[12] This may be particularly important with regard to agency interpretations that rely heavily on the ADA's legislative history since the Court in *Sutton* did not consider the legislative history finding that the statutory language was sufficient to support its holding.

Justice Stevens and Breyer dissented from the majority's opinions in *Sutton* and *Murphy* arguing that "in order to be faithful to the remedial purpose of the Act, we should give it a generous, rather than a miserly,

---

[12] EEOC Compliance Manual, Vol. 2, section 902, order 915.002,902-45 (1995).

construction." The dissenters found that the statutory scheme was best interpreted by looking only to the existence of an impairment that substantially limits an individual either currently or in the past since "this reading avoids the counterintuitive conclusion that the ADA's safeguards vanish when individuals make themselves more employable by ascertaining ways to overcome their physical or mental limitations."

DIRECT THREAT

Once an ADA employment case has advanced past the threshold question of whether the plaintiff is an individual with a disability, the next set of issues involve whether the individual can perform the essential functions of the job in question with or without reasonable accommodation. The qualifications standards used may also include a requirement that an individual shall not pose a direct threat to the health or safety of other individuals in the workplace.[13] Title III contains a similar provision stating that an entity does not have to permit an individual to participate in or benefit from the services of the entity where the individual poses a direct threat to the health or safety of others.[14]

In *Bragdon v. Abbott* the Court dealt with this issue in the title III (public accommodations) context and found that the ADA does not require that an entity permit an individual to participate in or benefit from the services of a public accommodation where such an individual poses a direct threat to the health or safety of others.[15] The Court determined that there is a duty to assess the risk of infection "based on the objective, scientific information available" and that a "belief that a significant risk existed, even if maintained in good faith, would not relieve him from liability." The Court remanded the case for consideration of the weight to be given to various pieces of evidence relating to the direct threat issue and on remand the court of appeals for the first circuit concluded that the defendant had produced no legitimate scientific evidence to show that providing routine dental care would subject him to a significant risk of contacting HIV.[16] The Supreme Court denied certiorari on May 24, 1999.[17]

---

[13] 42 U.S.C. §§12112-12113.

[14] 42 U.S.C. §12182(3).

[15] 42 U.S.C. §12182(b) (3).

[16] *Abbott v. Bragdon*, 163 F.3d 87 (1st Cir. 1998).

[17] 526 U.S. 1131 (1999).

Although the Court in *Albertsons, Inc. v. Kirkingburg* did not specifically address the direct threat language, it dealt with a related concept concerning federal safety regulations. In *Albertsons*, the Court held that an employer who requires an employee as part of a job qualification to meet applicable federal safety regulations does not have to justify enforcing those regulations, even if there is an experimental waiver program.

COMMUNITY PLACEMENT AND MENTALLY DISABLED INDIVIDUALS

In *Olmstead v. Georgia,*[18] the Supreme Court held that title II of the ADA requires states to place individuals with mental disabilities in community settings rather than institutions when the State's treatment professionals have determined that community placement is appropriate, community placement is not opposed by the individual with a disability, and the placement can be reasonably accommodated. "Unjustified isolation... is properly regarded as discrimination based on disability." The *Olmstead* case had been closely watched by both disability groups and state governments. Although disability groups have applauded the holding that undue institutionalization qualifies as discrimination by reason of disability, the Supreme Court did place certain limitations on this right. In addition to the agreement of the individual affected, the Court also dealt with the issue of what is a reasonable modification of an existing program and stated: "Sensibly construed, the fundamental-alteration component of the reasonable-modifications regulation would allow the State to show that, in the allocation of available resources, immediate relief for the plaintiffs would be inequitable, given the responsibility the State has undertaken for the care and treatment of a large and diverse population of persons with mental disabilities." This examination of what constitutes a reasonable modification may have implications for the interpretation of similar concepts in the employment and public accommodations titles of the ADA.

---

[18] 527 U.S. 581 (1999).

APPLICATION OF THE ADA TO STATE PRISONS

In *Pennsylvania Department of Prisons v. Yeskey,*[19] the Court found that state prisons were covered under tittle II of the ADA. The state had argued that state prisoners were not covered since such coverage would "alter the usual constitutional balance between the States and Federal Government." The Supreme Court rejected this argument, observing that "the ADA plainly covers state institutions *without* any exception that could cast the coverage of prisons into doubt."

COLLECTIVE BARGAINING AGREEMENTS

In *Wright v. Universal Maritime Service Corp.,*[20] a unanimous Court held that the general arbitration clause in a collective bargaining agreement does not require a plaintiff to use the arbitration procedure for an alleged violation of the ADA. The court's decision was limited since it did not find it necessary to reach the issue of the validity of a union-negotiated waiver. In other words, the Court found that a general arbitration agreement in a collective bargaining agreement is not sufficient to waive rights under civil rights statutes. The Court did not reach situations where collective bargaining agreements are very specific in requiring arbitration for alleged violations of civil rights statutes.

RECEIPT OF SSDI BENEFITS

In *Cleveland v. Policy Management Systems Corp.,* the Supreme Court unanimously held that pursuit and receipt of SSDI benefits does not automatically estop a recipient from pursuing an ADA claim or even create a strong presumption against success under the ADA.[21] Observing that the Social Security Act and the ADA both help individuals with disabilities but in different ways, the Court found that "despite the appearance of conflict that arises from the language of the two statutes, the two claims do not inherently conflict to the point where courts should apply a special negative presumption like the one applied by the Court of Appeals here." The fact that

---

[19] 524 U.S. 206 (1998).
[20] 525 U.S. 70 (1998).
[21] 526 U.S. 795 (1999).

the ADA defines a qualified individual as one who can perform the essential functions of the job with or without reasonable accommodation was seen as a key distinction between the ADA and the Social Security Act. In addition, the Court observed that SSDI benefits are sometimes granted to individuals who are working.

However, although these distinctions between the two statutes would rule out a special legal presumption, the Court did note that in some cases an earlier SSDI claim may genuinely conflict with an ADA claim. Therefore, if an individual has asserted that he or she is unable to work in an application for SSDI benefits, this may negate the ADA requirement that the individual with a disability be able to perform the essential functions of the job. For that reason the Court held that "an ADA plaintiff cannot simply ignore the apparent contradiction that arises out of the earlier SSDI total disability claim. Rather, she must proffer a sufficient explanation." Since the parties to the case in *Cleveland* did not have the opportunity to examine the plaintiff's contentions in court, the case was vacated and remanded for further proceedings.

ELEVENTH AMENDMENT ISSUES

On February 21, 2001, the Supreme Court decided *Garrett v. University of Alabama.*[22] In a 5-4 decision, the Court held that the Eleventh Amendment bars suits to recover monetary damages by state employees under title I of the Americans with Disabilities Act (ADA). Although the ruling is narrowly focused concerning the ADA, it has broad implications regarding federal-state power[23] and emphasizes the difficulty of drafting federal legislation under section 5 of the Fourteenth Amendment that will withstand Eleventh Amendment scrutiny.[24] In conclusion, the majority opinion stated that "Congress is the final authority as to desirable public policy, but in order to authorize private individuals to recover money damages against the States, there must be a pattern of discrimination by the States which violates the Fourteenth Amendment, and the remedy imposed by Congress must be

---

[22] For a more detailed discussion of *Garrett* see CRS Report RS20828, *University of Alabama v. Garrett: Federalism limits on the Americans with Disabilities Act,* by Nancy Lee Jones.

[23] For a detailed discussion of federalism see CRS Report RL30315, *Federalism and the Constitution: Limits on Congressional Power,* by Kenneth Thomas.

[24] It should also be observed that the Supreme Court did not address this issue in the cases it has already decided since it was not presented to the Court. *Pennsylvania Department of Corrections v. Yeskey, supra.* "This case, as it comes to us, presents no constitutional question." *Olmstead v. L.C., supra.*

congruent and proportional to the targeted violation. Those requirements are not met here...."[25] A strong dissent by Justice Breyer, joined by Justices Stevens, Souter and Ginsburg, argued that the majority ignored powerful evidence of discriminatory treatment.

---

[25] Slip op. at 16.

Chapter 13

THE AMERICANS WITH DISABILITIES ACT: ELEVENTH AMENDMENT ISSUES

Nancy Lee Jones

INTRODUCTION

The Supreme Court has granted certiorari and heard oral argument in *Garrett v. University of Alabama,* a case involving the application of the Eleventh Amendment to the Americans with Disabilities Act (ADA). *Garrett* is likely to be one of the most significant cases of the 2000-2001 Supreme Court term as it could have an impact on ADA coverage of states and localities and on the doctrine of federalism. This chapter will provide a brief overview of the Eleventh Amendment and its application to the ADA. It will be updated as appropriate.

SUPREME COURT INTERPRETATIONS OF THE ELEVENTH AMENDMENT

Although federalism was for many years largely ignored, starting in 1992 with *New York v. United States*[1] the Supreme Court began what some

---

[1] 505 U.S. 144 (1992).

commentators have referred to as a "rebirth of federalism."[2] A recent chapter in this "rebirth" involves a trio of cases from June 1999 where the Supreme Court expanded state sovereign immunity from suit under the Eleventh Amendment.[3] Essentially, these cases, combined with several from previous terms, limit the extent to which Congress can abrogate the state's sovereign immunity from suit. In other words, Congress may statutorily allow a state to be sued by individuals but this congressional power is limited.

The Eleventh Amendment states "The Judicial power of the United States shall not be construed to extend to any suit in law or equity, commenced or prosecuted against one of the United States by Citizens of another State, or by Citizens of Subjects of any Foreign State." The Supreme Court has found that the eleventh Amendment cannot be abrogated by the use of Article I powers but that section 5 of the Fourteenth Amendment can be used for abrogation in certain circumstances. Section 5 of the Fourteenth Amendment states: "The Congress shall have the power to enforce, by appropriate legislation, the provisions of this article."

The circumstances where section 5 of the Fourteenth Amendment can be used to abrogate the Eleventh Amendment were discussed in the recent Supreme Court decisions in *College Savings Bank v. Florida Prepaid Postsecondary Educ. Expense Board, supra, Florida Prepaid Postsecondary Educ. Expense Board v. College Savings Bank, supra,* and *Kimel v. Florida Board of Regents.*[4] They reiterated the principle that the Congress may abrogate state immunity from suit under the Fourteenth Amendment and found that there were three conditions necessary for successful abrogation.

---

[2] Curt A. Levey, "The Quiet Revolution Conservatives Continue Federalism Resurgence by Expanding State Immunity," 157 N.J.L.J. 707 (August 23, 1999). See also Thomas, "Federalism and the Constitution: Limits on Congressional Power," CRS Report RL30315.

[3] *Alden v. Maine,* 527 U.S. 706 (1999)(Congress lacks the authority when exercising Article I powers to subject non-consenting states to private suits for damages in state courts); *College Savings Bank v. Florida Prepaid Postsecondary Educ. Expense B.d.,* 527 U.S. 666(1999) (The Trademark Remedy Clarification Act, TRCA, which subjected states to suit for false and misleading advertising, did not validly abrogate state sovereign immunity; neither the right to be free from a business competitor's false advertising nor a more generalized right to be secure in one's business interests qualifies as a property right protected by the Due Process Clause); *Florida Prepaid Postsecondary Educ. Expense Bd. v. College Savings Bank,* 527 U.S. 627 (1999) (Congress may abrogate state sovereign immunity but must do so through legislation that is appropriate within the meaning of section 5 of the Fourteenth Amendment; Congress must identify conduct that violates the Fourteenth Amendment and must tailor its legislation to remedying or preventing such conduct).

[4] 528 U.S. 62 (2000).

- Congressional power is limited to the enactment of "appropriate" legislation to enforce the substantive provisions of the Fourteenth Amendment.

- The legislation must be remedial in nature.

- There must be a "congruence and proportionality" between the injury to be prevented and the means adopted to that end.

The clearest discussion of these conditions is found in *City of Boerne v. Flores*[5] where the Supreme Court held that Religious Freedom Restoration Act (RFRA) exceeded congressional power. In reaching its holding, the Court acknowledged that section 5 was a positive grant of legislative power to Congress. "Legislation which deters or remedies constitutional violations can fall within the sweep of Congress' enforcement power even if in the process it prohibits conduct which is not itself unconstitutional ...."[6] The grant of authority to Congress is not unlimited, however. Acknowledging that "the line between measures that remedy or prevent unconstitutional actions and measures that make a substantive change in the governing law is not easy do discern, and Congress must have wide latitude in determining where it lies," the Court emphasized that there must be a "congruence and proportionality between the injury to be prevented or remedied and the means adopted to that end."[7] In applying this analysis to factual situations, the Court compared and contrasted RFRA and the Voting Rights Act. Congress had before it a record of state voting laws passed due to bigotry when it passed the Voting Rights Act; the Court found no such record of religious persecution occurring during the past forty years examined during the enactment of RFRA. But even if there had been a stronger legislative record, the Court found that RFRA could not be considered remedial. "RFRA is so out of proportion to a supposed remedial or preventive object that it cannot be understood as responsive to, or designed to prevent, unconstitutional behavior."[8] The Court observed that RFRA would require a state to demonstrate a compelling interest and show that it has adopted the least restrictive means of achieving that interest, a test that "is the most demanding test known to constitutional law."[9]

---

[5] 521 U.S. 507 (1997).
[6] *Id.* at 518.
[7] *Id.* at 519-520.
[8] *Id.* at 532.
[9] *Id.* at 534.

The Supreme Court's decision in *Kimel* used the same reasoning advanced in its earlier Eleventh Amendment cases to conclude that the Age Discrimination in Employment Act (ADEA) contained a clear statement of congressional intent to abrogate the Eleventh Amendment but exceeded congressional authority under section 5 of the Fourteenth Amendment. The ADEA prohibits discrimination by an employer due to age and provides several exceptions, for example, where there is a "bona fide occupational qualification." In 1974 the ADEA was amended to extend its discrimination prohibition to the States.

Quoting extensively from *Boerne, supra,* the *Kimel* Court adhered to its conditions for abrogation limiting congressional power to (1) the enactment of "appropriate legislation," (2) remedial legislation, and (3) a "congruence and proportionality" between the injury to be prevented and the means adopted to that end. The ADEA requirements were not found to be "appropriate." The Court stated that "the substantive requirements the ADEA imposes on state and local governments are disproportionate to any unconstitutional conduct that conceivable could be targeted under the Equal Protection Clause."[10] Age classifications were not seen as "so seldom relevant to the achievement of any legitimate state interest that laws grounded in such considerations are deemed to reflect prejudice and antipathy."[11] In addition, the Court found, older persons have not been subjected to a "history of purposeful unequal treatment" and "old age does not define a discrete and insular minority because all persons, if they live out their normal life spans, will experience it."[12] As a consequence, the ADEA was found to prohibit "substantially more state employment decisions and practices than would likely be held unconstitutional under the applicable equal protection, ration basis standard."[13]

The ADA and Sovereign Immunity

The ADA cites to the Fourteenth Amendment as its constitutional basis,[14] specifically abrogates state immunity under the Eleventh Amendment[15] and thus would appear to meet the specificity required for

---

[10] *Kimel, supra,* at 18.

[11] *Id.* at 19 citing *Cleburne v. Cleburne Living Center,* 473 U.S. 432, 440 (1985).

[12] *Id.* at 19.

[13] *Id.* at 22.

[14] 42 U.S.C. §12101(b) (4).

[15] 42 U.S.C. §12202.

such a statement of abrogation by *Kimel.* The issue, then, is whether the other elements of a successful abrogation, as described by the Supreme Court in the cases discussed above, are present. The Supreme Court granted certiorari in two cases involving this issue, *Alsbrook v. City of Maumelle*[16] and *Florida Department of Corrections v. Dickson*,[17] but the cases were settled prior to oral argument.[18] However, the issue resurfaced when the Court granted certiorari in *Garrett v. University of Alabama.*[19]

In *Garrett,* the Eleventh Circuit held that the state was not immune from suits brought by state employees. The court of appeals decision involved two consolidated lawsuits by separate Alabama employees. One of these employees, Patrical Garret, had been undergoing treatment for breast cancer when, she alleged, she was transferred from her unit after being told that her boss did not like sick people. The second plaintiff, Milton Ash, alleged that the Alabama Department of Human Services did not enforce its non-smoking policy and that he was not able to control his asthma.[20] The district court held that the accommodation provisions of the ADA were not a valid exercise of Congress' enforcement power under the Fourteenth Amendment and thus Congress did not abrogate the Eleventh Amendment.[21] The Eleventh Circuit disagreed and held that states do not have Eleventh Amendment immunity from claims brought under the ADA. The majority did not provide a detailed analysis in this decision but rather referred to the Eleventh Circuit's decision in *Kimel* regarding the ADA and observed that "we, of course, are bound by the decision...." *Kimel,* as was discussed above, was decided by the Supreme Court but only regarding the ADEA claim; the Supreme Court did not address the ADA issue that had been before the Eleventh Circuit. The Supreme Court held oral argument in *Garrett* on October 11, 2000.

Garrett is one of the most closely watched cases in the 2000-2001 Supreme Court term and the likely outcome is not at all clear. The Courts of appeals had been split in their determinations prior to the Supreme Court's

---

[16] 68 U.S.L.W. 3478 (January 21, 2000).

[17] 2000 U.S. LEXIS 996 (January 25, 2000).

[18] 2000 U.S. LEXIS 1545 (Feb. 23, 2000). See Linda Greenhouse, "Justice Rebuff Inmate's Bid on Early Supervised Release," *The New York Times* A-18 (March 2, 2000).

[19] 68 U.S.L.W. 3649 (April 18, 2000).

[20] 9 BNA's Americans with Disabilities Act Manual 46, 47 (April 27, 2000).

[21] 989 F. Supp. 1409 (N.D. Ala. 1998).

decision in *Kimel* but court of appeals decisions since *Kimel* have found that the ADA does not properly abrogate the Eleventh Amendment.[22]

An examination of the statutory language and legislative history indicates that the ADA could meet the Court's abrogation requirements to be "appropriate" legislation, remedial, and have a "congruence and proportionality" between the injury to be prevented and the means adopted to that end. However, given the recent lack of success in abrogating the Eleventh Amendment, the Court's examples regarding race and sex, and the high standard for finding "congruence and proportionality," it is possible the Court would find that the ADA does not successfully abrogate the Eleventh Amendment.[23]

Appropriate Legislation to Enforce the Substantive Provisions of the Fourteenth Amendment

The ADA is a civil rights statute. It enforces constitutional standards to address the major areas of discrimination faced by individuals with disabilities and specifically invokes "the power to enforce the fourteenth amendment."[24] In *Cleburne v. Cleburne Living Center,*[25] the Supreme Court applied the Fourteenth Amendment to individuals with mental retardation and found that, although such individuals were not part of a suspect class, a zoning ordinance which excluded group homes from certain locations violated the Fourteenth Amendment. Expanding upon *Cleburne,* the ADA specifically finds that "individuals with disabilities are a discrete and insular minority who have been faced with restrictions and limitations, subjected to a history of purposeful unequal treatment, and relegated to a position of political powerlessness in our society, based on characteristics that are beyond the control of such individuals and resulting from stereotypic assumptions not truly indicative of the individual ability of such individuals to participate in, and contribute to, society."[26] The statement of findings and purposes and the legislative history of the ADA draw parallels to the

---

[22] See *Lavia v. Commonwealth of Pennsylvania,* 224 F.3d 190 (3d Cir. 2000); *Erickson v. Northeastern Illinois University,* 207 F.3d 945 (7th Cir. 2000); *Popovich v. Cuyahoga Country Court of Common Pleas,* 2000 U.S. App. LEXIS 23388 (September 18, 2000).

[23] It should be noted that although the Supreme Court has considered other cases under Title II of the ADA, the Eleventh Amendment issue was not addressed.

[24] 42 U.S.C. §12101(b) (4).

[25] 473 U.S. 432 (1985).

[26] 42 U.S.C. §12101(a) (7).

treatment of individuals with disabilities and racial minorities whose protection the Court has found to be within congressional authority.[27]

Remedial Legislation

The ADA would arguably meet the Supreme Court's requirement that the legislation be remedial in nature. Although there was some legislative history under the ADEA, it was determined by the Supreme Court in *Kimel* to be inadequate to fulfill the remedial requirement of successful abrogation. The record under the ADA is more extensive and includes statutory language, report language, and hearing testimony.

The ADA's statement of findings and purpose indicates that historical society has tended to isolate and segregate individuals with disabilities and notes that individuals with disabilities, unlike individuals who have experienced discrimination due to race, have often had no legal recourse to remedy such discrimination. The ADA states that its purpose is "to provide clear, strong, consistent, enforceable standards addressing discrimination against individuals with disabilities."[28] The instances of discrimination detailed in the hearings on the ADA and described in the House and Senate Reports also support the remedial nature of the legislation and specifically discuss the inadequacy of state laws.[29] For example, the House report states: "State laws are inadequate to address the pervasive problems of discrimination that people with disabilities are facing....Too many States, for whatever reason, still perpetuate confusion.... The fifty State Governor's Committees, with whom the President's Committee on Employment of People with Disabilities works, report that existing state laws do not adequately counter acts of discrimination against people with disabilities."[30]

---

[27] See, 42 U.S.C. §12101; Testimony of Sandy Parrino, quoted in S.Rept. 101-116, 101st Cong., 1st Sess. (1989).

[28] 42 U.S.C. §12101(b) (2).

[29] See S.Rept. 101-116, 101st Cong., 1st Sess. (1989); H.Rept. 101 – 485, Part 2, 101st Cong., 2d Sess.(1990).

[30] H.Rept.101-485, Part 2, 101st Cong., 2d Sess. 47 (1990), reprinted in 4 USCCAN 329 (1990). In addition to this report language, hearings on the ADA also contain testimony and studies which indicate discrimination against individuals with disabilities by states and localities. For example, testimony by Laura D. Cooper before the Subcommittee on Civil and Constitutional Rights of the House Judiciary Committee on the ADA gave several examples of discrimination she had experienced including inaccessible municipal buses and inaccessible voting places. "Americans with Disabilities Act of 1989," Hearings before the Subcommittee on Civil and Constitutional Rights, House Judiciary Committee (August 3, 1989), reprinted in 3 "Legislative History of Public Law 101-336 The Americans with Disabilities Act," Prepared for the House Committee on Education and

"Congruence and Proportionality" Between the Injury to be Prevented and the Means Adopted

The Supreme Court also requires that when Congress uses its power to abrogate state immunity by legislating pursuant to section 5 of the Fourteenth Amendment there must be a "congruence and proportionality" between the injury to be prevented and the means adopted. The finding of the inadequacy of existing remedies in both the statute and its legislative history combined with the remedies enacted by the ADA suggest a proportionality sufficient to meet the Supreme Court's requirements.

It could be argued that the requirement of the ADA for reasonable accommodations places a burden on employers and others that is inappropriate; however, the ADA also contains limitations on this requirement. For example, for the purpose of employment, an employer need not make an accommodation if he or she can demonstrate that the accommodation would impose an undue hardship on the operation of the business.[31]

Labor, 101ˢᵗ Cong., 2d Sess. (Dec. 1990), Serial No. 102-C at 1984. See also testimony regarding problems with police services, *Id.* at 1005, 1008, 1118, 1197; testimony regarding access to state courts, *Id.* at 1079; testimony regarding state hospitals, *Id.* at 1203; and testimony regarding state employment, *Id.* at 1225, 1247.

[31] 42 U.S.C. §12112(b)(5)(A).

Chapter 14

THE AMERICANS WITH DISABILITIES ACT: SUPREME COURT CASES 2001-2002 TERM

Nancy Lee Jones

INTRODUCTION

The Supreme Court granted certiorari in three cases involving the Americans with Disabilities Act (ADA), 42 U.S.C. §12101 *et seq.*, in the 2001-2002 Supreme Court term. The Supreme Court has decided *U.S. Airways Inc. v. Barnett* and *Toyota Motor Manufacturing, Kentucky Inc. v. Williams* but *Chevron U.S.A., Inc. v. Echazabal* is still pending. All three cases arose out of employment issues and the two decided cases have narrowed the scope of the ADA. *Echazabal* presents issues involving whether an individual is a "qualified individual with a disability" if there is a risk to the employee in performing the job. This report briefly discusses the decided cases and the pending decision in *Echazabal*. It will be updated as necessary.

U.S. AIRWAYS INC. V. BARNETT

The Supreme Court in *U.S. Airways v. Barnett*[1] held that an employer's showing that a requested accommodation by an employee with a disability conflicts with the rules of a seniority system is ordinarily sufficient to establish that the requested accommodation is not "reasonable" within the meaning of the ADA. The Court, in a majority opinion by Justice Breyer, observed that a seniority system, "provides important employee benefits by creating, and fulfilling, employee expectations of fair, uniform treatment" and that to require a "typical employer to show more than the existence of a seniority system might undermine the employees' expectations of consistent, uniform treatment." Thus, in most ADA cases, the existence of a seniority system would entitle an employer to summary judgment in its favor.

The Court found no language in the ADA which would change this presumption if the seniority system was imposed by management and not by collective bargaining. However, Justice Breyer found that there were some exceptions to this rule for "special circumstances" and gave as examples situations where (1) the employer "fairly frequently" changes the seniority system unilaterally, and thereby diminishes employee expectations to the point where one more departure would "not likely make a difference" or (2) the seniority system contains so many exceptions that one more exception is unlikely to matter.

Although the majority in *Barnett* garnered five votes, the Court's views were splintered. There were strong dissents and two concurring opinions. In her concurrence, Justice O'Connor stated that she would prefer to say that the effect of a seniority system on the ADA depends on whether the seniority system is legally enforceable but that since the result would be the same in most cases as under the majority's reasoning, she joined with the majority to prevent a stalemate. The dissents took vigorous exception to the majority's decision with Justice Scalia, joined by Justice Thomas, arguing that the ADA does not permit any seniority system to be overridden. The dissent by Justice Souter, joined by Justice Ginsburg, argued that nothing in the ADA insulted seniority rules from a reasonable accommodation requirement and that the legislative history of the ADA clearly indicated congressional intent that seniority systems be a factor in reasonable accommodations determinations but not the major factor.

---

[1] 2002 U.S. LEXIS 3034. 70 U.S.L.W. 4285 (April 29. 2002).

TOYOTA MOTOR MANUFACTURING V. WILLIAMS

The Supreme Court in *Toyota Motor Manufacturing v. Williams*[2] examined whether the plaintiff was an individual with a disability under the first prong of the definition of individual with a disability; that is, whether she had a physical or mental impairment that substantially limits a major life activity. There was no dispute regarding the fact that the plaintiff's carpal tunnel syndrome and tendinitis were physical impairments. The difference of opinion involved whether these impairments *substantially* limited the plaintiff in the major life activity of performing manual tasks. In order to resolve this issue, Justice O'Connor, writing for the unanimous Court, determined that the word substantial "clearly precluded impairments that interfere in only a minor way with the performance of manual tasks." Similarly, the Court found that the term "major life activity" "refers to those activities that are of central importance to daily life." Finding that these terms are to be "interpreted strictly,"[3] the Court held that "to be substantially limited in performing manual tasks, an individual must have an impairment that prevents or severely restricts the individual from doing activities that are of central importance to most people's daily lives." Significantly, the Court also stated that "[t]he impairment's impact must also be permanent or long-term." The Supreme Court's opinion emphasized the need for an individualized assessment of the effect of the impairment. Justice O'Connor found it insufficient to merely submit evidence of a medical diagnosis of an impairment; rather, the individual must offer evidence that the extent of the impairment in their own situation is substantial.[4]

CHEVRON U.S.A., INC. V. ECHAZABAL

The last ADA case remaining to be decided in the 2001-2002 term is *Chevron U.S.A., Inc. v. Echazabal.* In *Echazabal,* 226 F.3d 1063 (9th Cir.

---

[2] 534 U.S. 184 (2002).

[3] Confirmation of the need for strict interpretation was found by the Court in the ADA's statement of findings and purposes where Congress stated that "some 43,000,000 Americans have one or more physical or mental disabilities." [42 U.S.C. §12101(a)(1)] Justice O'Connor observed that "if Congress had intended everyone with a physical impairment that precluded the performance of some isolated, unimportant, or particularly difficult manual task to qualify as disabled, the number of disabled Americans would surely have been much higher."

[4] For a more detailed discussion of this decision see CRS Report RS21105, *The Americans with Disabilities Act: Toyota Motor Manufacturing v. Williams,* by Nancy Lee Jones.

2000), the ninth circuit determined that an employer violated the ADA by refusing to hire an applicant with a serious liver condition whose illness would be aggravated through exposure to the chemicals in the workplace. The ADA allows an employer to impose as a qualification standard that the individual shall not pose a direct threat to the health or safety of other individuals in the workplace[5] but does not discuss a threat to the individual's health or safety. However, the EEOC has interpreted the ADA to allow an employer to assert a direct threat defense to an allegation of employment discrimination where the threat is posed only to the health or safety of the individual making the allegation.[6]

The Supreme Court agreed to review *Echazabal* on October 29, 2001.[7] The issue before the Court is whether an individual who is unable to carry out the essential functions of the job without incurring significant risks to the individual's own health or life is a qualified individual who meets the qualification standards for the job. This issue has not been discussed in great depth in other opinions although the eleventh circuit has agreed with the EEOC that the direct threat defense encompasses threats to the individual alleging discrimination.[8] The Supreme Court has examined an analogous issue in *UAW v. Johnson Controls, Inc.*,[9] which held that under the Civil Rights Act of 1964 employers could not enforce "fetal protection" policies that kept women, whether pregnant or with the potential to become pregnant, from jobs that might endanger a developing fetus.

---

[5] 42 U.S.C. §12113.

[6] 29 C.F.R. §1630.15(b) (2).

[7] Cert. granted, 70 U.S.L.W. 3314 (Oct. 29, 2001); Case summary, 69 U.S.L.W. 3650 (April 3, 2001).

[8] *Moses v. American Nonwovens, Inc.*, 97 F.3d 446 (11th Cir. 1996).

[9] 499 U.S. 187(1991).

INDEX

A

W

Z

35⁰⁰
16x